P9-DTN-140

The Writer's I Ching: Wisdom for the Creative Life

The Writer's I Ching: Wisdom for the Creative Life

by
Jessica Page Morrell

RUNNING PRESS
PHILADELPHIA · LONDON

© 2007 by Jessica P. Morrell and Elaura Niles
All rights reserved under the Pan-American and International Copyright Conventions
Printed in Canada
This book may not be reproduced in whole or in part, in any form or by any means, electronic or
mechanical, including photocopying, recording, or by any information storage and retrieval system
now known or hereafter invented, without written permission from the publisher.

9 8 7 6 5 4 3 2 1
Digit on the right indicates the number of this printing

Library of Congress Control Number: 2007926351

ISBN-13: 978-0-7624-2547-1
ISBN-10: 0-7624-2547-4

Cover and interior design by Maria Taffera Lewis, Blue Studio Design
Typography: Perpetua and Futura

This book may be ordered by mail from the publisher.
Please include $2.50 for postage and handling.
But try your bookstore first!

Running Press Book Publishers
2300 Chestnut Street
Philadelphia, PA 19103-4371

Visit us on the web!
www.runningpress.com

Photo Credits:
Card photos © iStockphoto.com except for the following:
Hexagram 16: © Marc Muench/Stone/Getty Images
Hexagram 37: © Stuart Westmorland/Riser/Getty Images
Hexagram 38: © Skip Brown/National Geographic/Getty Images
Hexagram 42: © DAJ/Getty Images
Hexagram 54: © Robert Van Der Hilst/Stone/Getty Images

Acknowledgments

Books are never written without help.
Many thanks to Stephanie Kip Rostan, Jennifer Kasius and
Deb Grandinetti for guiding it along,
and to the many resources written about the I Ching.

Also, warm thanks to Bonnie and Mark Kittleson
for the loan of their beach house
where the ideas for this book came into being.

Dedication

To the sages who brought the *I Ching* to light
and the sages who now walk among us

Contents

Contents

Contents

Everything changes, everything stays the same.

—The Teachings of Buddha

Preface

In Carl Jung's introduction to Richard Wilhelm's translation of the *I Ching*, he explained that he'd never traveled to China and did not speak Chinese. I echo his admission, as well as his confession that he often found Eastern philosophies obscure and difficult to understand. But like Jung and many others through the centuries, in the *I Ching* I have found profound wisdom—and perhaps a friend.

I teach writers, coach writers, edit the work of writers, and am a writer. I juggle to keep many projects afloat, to inspire students, and to deliver the goods for clients. In all of these tasks and roles there are times when interactions, deadlines, or projects cause nerve-jangling anxiety or uncertainty. I have found that when I turn to the *I Ching* for guidance, it never lets me down and always provides some insight that I would not arrive at on my own.

I've been using tarot cards for about twenty-five years now and I've known Feng Shui masters, astrology wizards, and seers. Besides my use of the tarot, I've essentially been a dabbler in these other traditions, intimidated by the complexity of Eastern approaches or the mathematics of the stars. Instead, I learned how fiction and nonfiction works, and how to explain what I know to other writers. So it was with deep gratitude and surprise that I began using the *I Ching*. I cannot describe it in any other way except to say that it deeply, simply, and clearly speaks to me. And when I listen, I am calmed and strengthened by what I learn.

—*Jessica Morrell*

One: Connecting

For me, writing is discovery.

—James Miller

If writing were easy, everyone would be doing it. The fact is, writing is difficult. It means finding the courage to commit your thoughts, emotions, and insights to the page, hoping to connect with readers, yet secretly fearing your reader's reactions and often doubting your ability to say what needs to be said. This fear is why so many writers disguise memoirs, buried dreams, obsessions, and failed relationships with fiction's closet of costumes.

Another reason that writing is difficult is that at any given moment a writer's mind is jumbled with images, memories, and dreams. The story in front of him presents a dizzying array of possibilities. Choices and decisions erupt at each turn: how to bring his protagonist to life while differentiating her from the rest of the cast of characters; how to illustrate the underlying theme of the novel and connect it to the premise. On a smaller scale, every word on every page must be weighed so that it is perfect, succinct, and evocative. In fact, at every juncture a writer analyzes and questions the words, images, and techniques he's using, and wonders if he's chosen wisely.

Meanwhile, emotions, like storm fronts, skitter across his or her mind, ranging from elation to despair. Delusions surface and are battled. Doubts and fears threaten to sabotage the project. As the story progresses, mysteriously, energy can falter.

Yet despite these difficulties, writing is not all suffering. It also brings connection and happiness, even moments of elation and giddiness, because writing is a process of discovery. Writers are like the early explorers who traveled afar, discovered new worlds, and then brought the wonders of these places home. But those daring steps into the unknown cannot be accomplished while holding your breath or waging a battle within. They are accomplished with your heart open, your mind focused, and your emotions calmed.

And as any explorer knows, it's easy to get lost.

But there is a way to work despite this storm, this cacophony of inner voices that sometimes drowns out the story that you're trying to write. You see, a writer must work from a place of calm, but at the same time, her mind needs permission to roam. To imagine what it's like to be a character living in another century or what the future is like on Mars. Or to simply slip into the past of her childhood and remember that world, recall the acute joys and pains of the child within.

So how is this accomplished?

Enter the *I Ching*, with its elegant solutions, uncanny accuracy, and ancient wisdom. Developed over centuries, it can serve as a compass, revealing not only fresh insights and practical advice, but also a new world. The way is shown and light is shed on current conditions, past events, and upcoming possibilities.

Enter next into the picture a writer living in Portland, Oregon. As I studied the *I Ching* and applied its jewel-like answers to everyday life, I began to see a connection between it and the process of writing. The next step seemed a natural one: to commingle the *I Ching* with the writing life. With practice, I discovered that it could be applied to a range of issues plaguing writers no matter the genre they're writing in. Thus, *The Writer's I Ching* came into being.

Like the original, it is a powerful tool. I've harnessed wisdom that was honed over centuries to solve problems, find balance, and understand ourselves better. Because understanding of the words on the page begins with knowing the self and working from a place of calm.

Two: The Sages Speak

In dwelling, live close to the ground.
In thinking, keep to the simple.
In conflict, be fair and generous.
In governing, don't try to control.
In work, do what you enjoy.
In family life, be completely present..

—Tao Le Ching

Ever since the beginning of humankind, we have tried to understand and explain the world around us. The West defined the world according to increasingly sophisticated science, data, and complicated reasoning. The Western mind-set leans toward logic, reason, and analysis. The Chinese, on the other hand, saw the world simply, drawing insights from nature and basic elements. Instead of reason, they used intuition and looked inward. Their emphasis was on finding balance, as water finds its resting place. Over the centuries, an Eastern philosophy emerged that was aimed at finding peace, balance, and purpose.

Many of the messages found in the *I Ching* (pronounced Ee Jing) are subtle, and refer to decidedly non-Western ways of dealing with life such as yielding, reflecting, or biding your time. At the heart of the philosophy is the understanding that there is an inherent energy in all things, especially in nature. The *I Ching* teaches us that wisdom is evolving, a living thing—that change is part of everything.

Most often, the *I Ching* is referred to as "the book of changes," with the title suggesting how this wisdom works. It is based on the natural world: its seasons, cycles, energies, and contradictions. The inspiration for its teachings comes from observing water, weather, stars, tides, animals, and plants. It also draws on basic elements such as fire and thunder, wood and metal. This understanding is elemental, grounded, and yet sophisticated because the forces found in nature are subtle, ever changing, and continuous.

The observations are also based on interactions among people—lovers, families, coworkers, and governments. It covers the most basic questions: how to be virtuous, generous, and honest. How to achieve ambitions and how to resolve conflicts. How to live with a peaceful heart. Or, how to remain courageous or focused when the odds are stacked against success.

History of the *I Ching*

Societies have always used methods of prophecy, with traditions such as astrology dating back to the beginnings of human existence. The origins of the *I Ching* are obscured by time, so there is both a historical and mythical interpretation of how it came about. No one knows the exact date it began because it was first an oral tradition. Early records of divination practices in ancient China depict heating animal bones in a fire and then examining the cracks that form to determine meaning. Tortoise shells were also heated, creating patterns that the inquirer would interpret. At some point, ancient questioners started carving symbols into the shells to record what had been asked and revealed. Methods of divination were used for all sorts of reasons—to ask if a prince would be born, to question the wisdom of a marriage, or to solve political issues.

During the Shang Dynasty (1766–1122 BCE) priests in the court predicted the future by applying hot metal pokers to discarded tortoise shells and then reading the cracks. From this practice evolved the *I Ching*, which is a sacred text credited to the "four sage theory," meaning that four of China's greatest minds were involved in its creation. It began with Fu Hsi, the king of China who lived sometime in third millennium BCE. According to legend, he was sitting near a river meditating on the meaning of life when a tortoise emerged from the water. Based on markings on its shell, he developed mathematical patterns called trigrams.

Centuries later, the next sage who influenced the *I Ching* was Wen Wang, king of the Chou, who was imprisoned by the Shang emperor. While captive around 1140 BCE, he meditated on the trigrams and wrote essays that depicted them as 64 hexagrams. These essays were said to have been written on prison walls, expanding the philosophy. He was eventually freed by his son, the Duke of Chou (1004 BCE), who began the new Chou dynasty. The Duke of Chou finished his father's work by writing further on the six lines within each hexagram.

It is said that Confucius (551–479 BCE) studied the text and added commentary to it. Some scholars question this theory and claim that the philosopher Lao-tzu compiled the text in the sixth century. Although its authorship has been lost to antiquity, what is known is that it influenced many Chinese philosophers and that Confucius and imperial scholars wrote the *Ten Wings,* a collection of commentaries about using the oracle to understand the world.

Over time the yarrow stalk, a common plant, was introduced as a means to ask and interpret questions, replacing bones and tortoise shells. Fifty yarrow stalks were drawn to form mathematical patterns that could be interpreted by consulting the corresponding hexagram. The yarrow stalks, which were readily available in China, made working with the *I Ching* easier and more accessible to more people.

By 500 BCE, after the Chou dynasty collapsed, we know that commoners were consulting the oracle. Now, the *I Ching* was the province not only of the emperor or royal court, but of anyone who could read. This was also a time of political upheaval and turmoil; the texts were collected into a book and diviners would travel the countryside carrying them. In about 221 BCE the new rulers, the Ch'in Dynasty, came into power and ordered all books burned. However, because of the *I Ching's* practical value, copies of it were spared. The Han dynasty followed and in its more stable and peaceful society, the *I Ching* became a revered object of scholarly study and was gradually expanded.

A number of contemporary people have also contributed to our knowledge of the *I Ching*. Richard Wilhelm, who lived in China for twenty years, translated it into German in 1931. The first sentence of his translation begins: "The Book of Changes—*I Ching* in Chinese—is unquestionably one of the most important books in the world's literature." During his years in China he studied with the sage and scholar Lao Nai-hsuan. After returning to Europe, Wilhelm became friends with Carl Jung, who was said to have studied the oracle for thirty years. Jung wrote the introductions to Wilhelm's *I Ching* and also *Secret of the Golden Flower*, which offered modern readers a deeper understanding of its teachings. Many contemporary books on the subject are based on Wilhelm's translations.

The *I Ching* meets the writing life

What does the *I Ching* bring to the writing process?

Counsel. We all have doubts. And writers, who need to constantly assess, analyze, and question their work, need to overcome these doubts. But before you can wrestle with doubt or with a specific problem, you must first recognize it. Your next step is deciding how to deal with it. Life, and especially the writing life, is slippery, sometimes overwhelming, and you constantly need to make adjustments. Luckily, the *I Ching* helps you focus and nudges you toward solutions using your innate understanding. With this knowledge, the weight of indecision is lifted and you can take action.

Peace of mind. The wisdom needed for a given situation is always available, but first you must discern if it lies within or can be found in the knowledge of experts. Part of the problem with finding solutions is that there is so much information about writing these days and sometimes it is contradictory. One expert claims to avoid using flashbacks in your novel, while another advises that flashbacks are an appropriate means to shed light on a character's motivation. And all the knowledge that you've gleaned in a lifetime or is available in the larger world doesn't necessarily answer every question. You need a method to match your many questions with appropriate answers. The traditional *I Ching* and *The Writer's I Ching* serve as a s p o t l i g h t , illuminating or pairing answers with questions. Once you realize that solutions are available, your fears and quandaries fade.

Confidence. Many times, a voice from within whispers instructions for your next steps, suggesting, for example, solutions to plot problems or your protagonist's secrets. But it's also nice to have a bit of reinforcement. *The Writer's I Ching* helps you listen to your intuition and pay attention to the quietest suggestions. This clarity keeps you on course.

Three: The Way

The universe is one great kindergarten for man.
Everything that exists has brought with it
its own peculiar lesson.
The mountain teaches stability and grandeur;
the ocean immensity and change.
Forests, lakes, and rivers, clouds and winds,
stars and flowers, stupendous glaciers and
crystal snowflakes-every form of animate
or inanimate existence,
leaves its impress upon the soul of man.

—Orison Swett Marden

Understanding that life is change and coping with change are at
the heart of the *I Ching* philosophy, comforting every writer who
has ever struggled with his craft. The universe and the conditions in your life
are constantly forming, transforming, and reforming. The ancient Chinese
sought a path that led through these changes, a way of moving in the world
that was fluid and yielding—they called this path the Tao.

The Tao (pronounced dow), or the way, has been translated and studied
extensively because it speaks in whispers with both simplicity and complexity.
It encourages you to live in wonder, noticing the world slipping from day to
night, season to season, an ever-changing miracle. And this sort of awareness
and wonder is a huge asset to writers.

In nature, the Tao is made visible—in flowing rivers, mystical waterfalls, brilliant starlight, and the flight of birds. The Tao also suggests that there is a duality in nature and in all things, along with ceaseless movement, ebb and flow. If your circumstances are now bad, be patient, because the other side of fortune will return. Morning always arrives after night, spring after a hard winter. It is all change and the I Ching teaches you to be a partner with change.

Yin and Yang

Yin and yang are the primary dual forces of nature and are the starting point for the teachings of the I Ching. They are not opposites, but complementary. Yin is earth; yang is sky. Yin is dark; yang is light.

Yin is the force that is related to the moon, the female, water, even numbers, night, soft, cold, wet, winter, and shadows. Yin yields and is relaxed. It also represents things that are moist, secretive, withdrawn, and receptive. Yin influences you to respond and says that the wise person pays attention to his inner voice and seeks stability. The power of yin comes from using your intuition, common sense, and instincts.

Yang is related to heaven, sun, the male, odd numbers, creativity, light, day, dry, summer, and sun. Yang is resistant, tense, and hard. Its energy is hot, bright, bold, and active. Yang influences push you outward, demanding physical release, effort, and activity. Yang helps you channel energy outward and into goals you want to accomplish.

The Eight Energies

Once you understand yin and yang as essential energies found in the world, then you can begin expanding your understanding of how they work in your own life and are the foundations for the I Ching. Formed from aspects of yin and yang, the Eight Energies are the building blocks of the I Ching. These eight symbols, first seen on a tortoise's shell thousands of years ago, are called trigrams because each is composed of three lines, either solid (?━━) or broken (━ ━). The solid lines represent yang, while the broken lines represent yin. In the trigrams, combinations of yin and yang energies or principles create all that happens in the universe. The yang lines refer to qualities that are strong, firm, unyielding, persistent, and enduring. The yin lines suggest

Archetype	Associations	Tao Principles	Flow	Chinese Name	Symbol
Wind	Penetrating, Often soft and gentle Early Summer, Northwest	Support and grow things to maturity	Yin	Sun	
Fire	Sun, Quick, Cling together, Summer, South	See and understand	Yin	Li	
Lake	Open waters, Serene, Freedom from restraint, Autumn, West	Exchange ideas	Yin	Tui	
Earth	Receptive grounded womb, nourishing, Early Autumn, Southwest	Make thoughts visible, Bring forth	Yin	K'un	
Mountain	Keeping still, Bound Early Spring Northeast	Understand what you know	Yang	Ken	
Water	Rushing water, Momentum taking risks, Winter, North	Focus Confront, Move forward	Yang	K'an	
Thunder	Exciting, Arousing Volatile, Spring, East	Strength to handle difficulties	Yang	Chen	
Heaven	Creative, Dynamic, Dragon, Shape changer, Early Winter, Northwest	Creativity coupled with strength	Yang	Chi'en	

suppleness, flexibility, adaptability, and yielding. Because these energies are found in nature, they are easy to understand and memorize.

The three lines that make up each trigram have symbols, associations, and elements of nature that reveal their essence. Next, let's look at the qualities that are found in these energies so that you can understand their influences in our daily lives. The eight energies are heaven, lake, fire, thunder, wind, water, mountain, and earth. It is easy to see how the ancient Chinese would have observed them in the natural world and reached conclusions about how these forces influence humankind.

Ch'ien: Heaven

Heaven stands for the strongest yang energy and connotes dragon power, dynamic energy, and authority. Heaven is infinite, an amazing source of creativity. It also stands for strength, steadiness, power, force, and good luck. In issues relating to politics, power struggles, or business, it can also refer to decisions, authority, and rules that can be oppressive or unfair. However, since heaven has an amazing influence on your earthly life, this trigram chiefly stands for potency. Contemplate new goals and directions under its influence and call on your inner resources to achieve them. Consider also challenging authority at this time, especially when regulations are unjust or constricting.

Associations: *Father, northwest, winter*

Tui: Lake

Some *I Ching* interpretations call this trigram open water, wetland, or marsh. It is yin and relates to the moon and its potent and often mysterious influences. The lake is a nurturing environment, a place where you can experience openness, happiness, pleasure, and even excess. There is a great sociability in the lake, a mingling with friends, an ease of belonging, and an easy exchange of ideas. Although the lake is a friendly, nurturing place, when it is opposed you tend toward antisocial behaviors—withdrawal, exile, moodiness, and distancing. The lake reminds you to use its nurturing waters to refresh and bolster the spirit, to feel energized by its depths.

Associations: *Youngest Daughter, west, autumn*

Li: Fire

Fire is a yang force, quick, active, and mighty. Fire needs fuel to survive and can be easily doused by water or aroused by wind. With this in mind, your inner fire can be squelched by emotions, doubts, anger, or outward constraints and situations. It can refer to fiery passions and emotions; it also represents illumination, awareness, clarity, intelligence, attachment, and dependence. Fire also relates to the sun and its powerful radiance. In a reading, it is a reminder to rekindle your passions, connect with your insights and emotions, and pursue your goals.

Associations: *Middle Daughter, south, summer*

Chen: Thunder

Thunder is yin and signifies change, as the weather sometimes swiftly changes. The qualities of thunder are movement, drive, awakening, activity, growth, and jolting energy. Thunder is especially helpful when you need to be engaged, think on your feet, and make quick decisions. As in all the trigrams, there is a duality at work here, because if you plunge headlong into action without contemplation or consultation, you can make serious mistakes.

Associations: *Oldest Son, east, spring*

Sun: Wind

The yang properties of the wind can be beneficial in your affairs since it can penetrate, but can also have a gentle impact, like a soft breeze on a spring day. So this trigram speaks of graceful efforts, along with ambition and motivation. The flip side of the wind is destructive weather—hurricanes, typhoons, and tornadoes. The significance here is that ambition and motivation can be on overload, fueled by greed or other negative motivations. A lack of wind in your life causes boredom and lethargy and reminds you to connect with friends and family to be reinvigorated.

Associations: *Oldest Daughter, southeast, summer*

K'an: Water

This element is the spirit of rushing water and forward movement. Yet water also has profound and deep influences in your affairs and in nature. As oceans and lakes have great and mysterious depths, so can your mind. Water is yin and suggests fluidity and a mindset that is flexible and contemplative. Water is also nurturing and sustaining. Because it also has great power, as seen in waterfalls, and at times can rage destructively in floods, it must be controlled. Thus, soul-searching and meaningful insights along with sometimes mysterious, perilous, and risky aspects are part of water.

Associations: *Middle Son, winter, north*

Ken: Mountain

The mountain is strongly yang, displaying strength and power in its huge mass. The mountain signifies calm, stillness, and forces that are immobile, resting, and meditating. The mountain relates to your emotional stability, your ability to remain calm, balanced thoughts, and deep convictions about justice and matters of conscience. The mountain is fair and can be trusted. If the mountain is unstable, great destruction such as an avalanche can result. When this happens, injuries, damage, and danger are possible. An unstable mountain influence operating in a person can lead to worry, isolation, and emotional instability.

Associations: *Youngest Son, spring, northeast*

K'un: Earth

The yin qualities of the earth in this trigram are magnified, since it is re-lated to water, moon, and females. It relates to even numbers, secrecy, and mystery, yet is nurturing and supportive. The earth, a generous mother, is re-ceptive, yielding, compliant, loyal, and responsive. The earth qualities in a person make him a good listener, someone with compassion and gentleness who also possesses tremendous inner strength. For like the earth, this per-son has the inner resources to bring forth creativity and life itself, as evidenced by blossoms and whole forests of magnificence.

Associations: *Mother, autumn, southwest*

Let's recap for a moment: yin and yang are the basis for understanding the universe; and the Tao is the fundamental flow in all things. The tao teaches us that all things in the universe are ever-changing and fluid. In the lives of mankind, this also reflects how our plans change and our dreams change along with tides, weather, and seasons. Besides our understanding that change is the essence of living, we've learned that energies and principles in the natural world can be understood and can influence the situations of everyday life.

Four: The Writer's Path

*I read and walked for miles at night along the beach,
writing bad blank verse and searching endlessly
for someone wonderful who would step out of the darkness
and change my life. It never crossed my mind
that that person could be me.*

—Anna Quindlen

While much is said about the difficulties of the writing life, it is also a great privilege and joy to spend our lives creating stories. Few people have the opportunity to spend hours immersed in a task so absorbing and rewarding. But the writing life is a mixed bag. For every moment of brilliance, there is an equal moment of worry. For every triumph, a pitfall. *The Writer's I Ching* is designed to help you with the many areas where trouble can erupt; provide a deeper understanding of techniques; and give you a broader perspective about the milestones you pass on the route to creative success.

But an oracle or sacred text cannot do the work for you. You must show up for the page, day after day, and continually hone your skills. The writing path requires stamina, persistence, and practical approaches to the many problems that you face. Consider the following suggestions as part of the writing path:

Set production goals. Production goals require that you're honor-bound to yourself. This means you'll find a way to measure your goals by counting words, hours, or pages in a set amount of time. Days, weeks, and months can slip by and become years if you don't set goals and make solid plans to achieve them. John Grisham wrote his first books while working seventy-plus hours a week. His goal was to pen one, legal-sized page each day. You know the rest of the story. Stephen King writes 1,500 words every day except for his birthday, the Fourth of July, and Christmas. If you complete one page each day, you will have a book written and edited within a year.

Devise a sensible routine. Write during your peak hours. Quit when you're tired, but don't quit because you give up. Find your own rhythms, methods, and rewards. William Hefferman advises: "Always stop the day's work when you know exactly what your next paragraph will be when you start up again the next day. It keeps one from the frustration of starting the day staring at a blank page. And it also keeps your mind churning, analyzing and 'writing' even after you've put down the pen, typewriter, computer, or whatever."

Another aspect of a writing routine that most of us don't consider is that when you write at the same time day after day, this practice signals the many layers of your consciousness that it's time for creativity and productivity, and it becomes easier to write during these times. A writing routine is also sooth-ing: a time alone you can return to again and again, your place away from the distractions of the world, your place amid the spinning planct.

Write because you love to write. Not because your best friend claims that you write amusing emails or a college professor liked your essay on Hawthorne. And certainly not because you imagine it's glamorous or a sure ticket to guest star on *Oprah!* If you don't enjoy most parts of the process, in-cluding editing and marketing, chances are you won't accomplish much. While some people approach writing half heartedly or don't write for readers, this book is especially written for those who are serious about improving the craft and being published. If you're interested in getting published, you need to in-vest time, energy, and study. Writing isn't for dabblers or dilettantes; it's a path for people who are called to it.

Abandon your excuses and instead develop habits of strength. There may never be a perfect time to write, and demands on your time will always pull you away from your desk. Your kitchen will always need cleaning. Your body will always need a workout, your dog will grow restless, and your paperwork will pile up. Write anyway, despite your excuses. If you're serious about your writing goals it is likely that you'll need to sacrifice another activity to make room for writing. Perhaps you'll watch less television, spend less time at the mall, or chat less on the phone. The writing life requires commitment and time. Ralph Peters admonishes us, "There are no shortcuts—no substitutes for experience and hard work. Roll up those sleeves, pal!"

Cultivate your skills. Writing is a lifelong endeavor, a craft that can always be improved and rediscovered. Never stop learning techniques and the business of getting published. Learn how to infuse tension in your writing, how to craft tight dialogue, how to unfold the backstory so that it illuminates the front story. But remember that your craft always begins word by word and every word must have a job to do in every sentence. If not, get rid of them. Collect vivid verbs, write in the active voice, and limit your use of modifiers. Consider Robert Jordan's advice on what a writer needs to know: "A knowledge of the structure of a sentence and the proper use of the English language. I have lost count of the times I've seen the flow of a story spoiled by an ugly sentence, and the times that what was printed could not possibly have been what the writer (or editor) thought was meant."

Live with deep awareness. Life presents endless opportunities for writers. The world brims with interesting people and events that intrigue you with their mysteries and tragedies. Fascinating strangers gossip at the next table, a sad-eyed woman strolls past and you wonder at her obvious sorrow. You hurry through the airport and spot a dozen stories in the lobby; even your fellow passengers' luggage seems to scream a message. It's been said that a writer is someone on whom nothing is lost. Keep your heart, eyes, and ears open. Notice, listen, take notes, and borrow from brimming life. Morley Callaghan once said, "There is only one trait that makes the writer. He is always watching." Let's add listening to Callaghan's statement—because writers constantly have an ear cocked for amusing tidbits, gaffes, straight-to-the-heart truths, and expressions that bring a person into sharp focus.

Read widely and critically. Richard Steel once said that reading is to the mind what exercise is to the body. You likely came to writing through your love of reading. Perhaps reading enchanted you, was a vehicle that transported you far from your everyday world. Return again and again for the voyage. Writers must be constant and omnivorous readers. Never feel guilty about time spent reading; the rhythms and music of language, mysteries of structure and storytelling will somehow slip into your consciousness as you read.

But don't expect an author's craft to slip into your understanding by some kind of osmosis. As you read, analyze the writer's skill. Notice verbs and metaphors and unusual word combinations. Notice how many chapters the author uses to tell a complicated story. Notice when he uses cliffhangers and what unanswered questions hang over the story. Notice the specific details he uses to shape characters and setting. Ask yourself about the themes found in the story and what techniques you can emulate.

Stephen King writes, "Constant reading will pull you into a place (a mindset, if you like the phrase) where you can write eagerly and without self-consciousness. It also offers you a constantly growing knowledge of what has been done and what hasn't, what is trite and what is fresh, what works and what just lies there dying (or dead) on the page."

Join the tribe. Writers are a rare tribe. We stand witness to the raptures and horrors around us. So answer the call and write because you were born to write. And write because following your birthright leads to bliss.

Choose writing and good things will follow. Notice how when you write regularly you simply feel more alive, more in sync with all the parts of yourself. Your life runs better when you're writing. You like yourself more. You feel more in touch with your soul. You feel more connected to the planet.

Five: The Bridge

Ask, and it shall be given you; seek and ye shall find;
knock, and it shall be opened unto you.

—Matthew 7:8

As writers we face dozens of decisions every day, both on the page and in our lives. At times, the questions seem unending: What is the theme of this essay? How can I reveal the inner turmoil of my protagonist? How can I find more time to write? Which project should I write first? What is stopping me from achieving my dreams?

The good news is that within you, or somewhere in the greater world, lie the answers you need. The bad news is that you're often deaf to these answers. Typically, a writer's mind swirls with trivia, images, and a torrent of story ideas. But when you sit down to solve a problem on the page, the sheer volume of all these images and data can obscure the solution.

The Writer's I Ching creates the bridge that provides the single answer when you most need it. It also helps you make difficult decisions, lessens the anxiety that occurs naturally when change takes place in your life, and strengthens intuition. *The Writer's I Ching* can also be consulted for sticky situations that occur in the writing life, such as how to handle relationship conflicts and the politics of getting published.

These consultations are made by drawing a card from the *The Writer's I Ching* deck and then reviewing the meaning of the hexagram that is depicted on the card and applying the answer to your situation. Each hexagram consists of two, three line configurations and each describes a state of being, a process, or a specific location where a person finds himself on the path of life. Yet each hexagram of the *I Ching* is more than a picture or chapter heading. It represents a snapshot of the energy or circumstances around you, as well as your unconscious, and is a means to evaluate your options for proceeding or thinking about a situation. Each is an insightful portrait of the underlying elements or the interplay that exists among different aspects of your situation.

However, a bit of warning here. The *I Ching*, nor any kind of guidance or oracle is a quick fix or a substitute for your own common sense. Neither the *I Ching* nor any oracle can reveal the future because it is always uncertain and changeable. But it can provide what is called a "working prophecy" to help you create a desirable future. And, of course, it's invaluable for helping you see deep into the present moment and understand the attributes of this time. The *I Ching* is for people who are proactive, interested in shaping their own destiny. It helps you to observe patterns in your life and know yourself better, as well as avoid danger, affirm a direction, or act on an opportunity.

You can also use the *I Ching* as a method for staying focused, accurate, and consistent. It is a powerful tool for mediation because it offers insights into the forces that lie within the questioner. It is particularly useful to consult it about timing, because business affairs or affairs of the heart often can best be acted upon when the time is ripe. It can be consulted to inquire whether the energy around a project or undertaking is supercharged or quiet. Is it time to make a move, or lie low? Should you reach out to those in authority, or bide your time? Is patience called for, or should you send out your manuscript?

Traditionally, the *I Ching* was consulted via a system of counting fifty yarrow stalks, a complicated process. Other divination methods have been used over the years, including beads, plants, and coins. Using coins is a fairly simple method, but I have found that a deck with images and symbols that penetrate the senses is an especially helpful tool for writers. Thus, *The Writer's I Ching* was created to provide succinct yet potent images and messages based on ageless principles.

The *I Ching*, like the wisdom found in ancient cultures around the world, was depicted in symbols and archetypes. As writers, we know that many stories and characters are evolved from archetypes and symbols. Most of us first encountered archetypes in the bedtime stories and fairy tales of childhood. We met wizards and wise men and magical beings, then tiptoed into a forbidden forest, holding our breath at its dangers. The reason writers use archetypes is simple: archetypes are clearly, deeply, and easily understood because they have always been part of storytelling. However, stories using archetypes were also developed as road maps to show the way through life's journey and to teach us how to deal with major life transitions and other challenges.

Symbols are also a bridge to the unconscious where memories and dreams and hopes reside. We know that in our lives symbols such as flags, or the swastika, or a Christmas tree all have layers of significance. Similarly, the symbols in the *I Ching* have layers of meaning that we can tap into. The *I Ching* was developed as a means to translate the archetypes and symbolism of ancient China into teachings that we can all understand and benefit from.

The symbols or hexagrams of the *I Ching* give you the means to access your inner guide and thus shape your destiny. *The Writer's I Ching* creates a bridge between the everyday world and the infinite world of symbolic language.

Over the centuries, people have concocted a variety of methods of divination, but in all methods and cultures, there exist three constants. First, there is the person asking the question. Second, there is someone who answers: a being, a generous, helping spirit, or a link to the unconscious or intuition that is our inner guidance. Third, there is a system of symbols created for interpreting the answer.

There is another aspect at work here too: to use the *I Ching* it is necessary, in those moments of questioning, to surrender control and allow a force beyond your everyday knowing to enter. This is similar to what happens every night when you sleep and surrender to the world of dreams, the magic of night. And this surrender, or perhaps we can call it trust, allows fate to play a hand in your life.

However, before using *The Writer's I Ching* to address your questions and problems with writing, there are a few a things to keep in mind.

Facing the future

The *I Ching* can be relied on to reveal the truth about your present situation. It does not predict an inevitable future while you wait passively and helplessly for events to unfold. The reason is simple: there is no such thing as a preordained future. Individual free will creates it. Your decisions, choices, and actions direct the future, and no means of divination can replace these aspects. But the beauty of working with *The Writer's I Ching* is that it can help you meet the future prepared, empowered and informed. But first comes asking.

Asking

Most people use the *I Ching* to help cope with difficult situations, or suggest a strategy for dealing with a specific issue. It is especially effective for understanding the underlying or surrounding influences such as when you have an important meeting looming or a crucial choice to make. You do not approach an *I Ching* reading as you would read a newspaper astrology column. It is not a game and should not be used frivolously. Any kind of divination, when approached with the proper attitude, is a means to place yourself in a world that offers wisdom, affirmation, and consolation.

The *I Ching* is traditionally *not* used for a yes-or-no question, or for choosing a direction at a crossroad. Questions such as "Will my agent call me this week?" that require a yes-or-no answer are not appropriate for the *I Ching*.

It provides guidance, a means of introspection, not Magic 8 Ball answers. Remember that you're bringing the power and wisdom of nature, spirituality, and possibility into play. Ask appropriate questions.

Sincerity, openness, and of willingness to learn are necessary attitudes for consulting the oracle. Always treat the cards and process with respect, handle them with care, and treat the information as if you're listening to a wise and trusted mentor. When you ask the *I Ching* about your writing, you'll likely be working on a specific project at the time. But remain open to suggestions that you need to work in other areas or take a completely different approach. Sometimes possibilities won't open up until you solve problems in your personal life. Or a writing goal will remain elusive until you've tamed your ego. Sometimes the answers don't seem to make sense at the time, but will make sense later when you look back at the circumstances. Sometimes you won't like the advice. Many times the *I Ching* provides answers with a startling clarity.

Asking a question of the *I Ching* is fairly simple when you use the deck provided. However, although this method was created for the ease of its use, it still requires that you treat the deck containing the hexagrams, as well as the questions and answers as all people have used the *I Ching* throughout the centuries—with respect, seriousness, and an open mind.

There are several important steps to an effective reading:

1. Focus. Approach the reading with calm, focus, and intention. It's often suggested that you wash your hands or perform some small ritual before touching the *I Ching* tools. Some people prefer to light a candle. Whatever means you use, the idea is to prepare your mind and emotions so that you can understand the information that is being revealed and then apply it to the situation. As best you can, quiet your mind and concentrate on the essence of your question. If you feel extremely distracted or troubled, sometimes it's best to wait before asking a question. The *I Ching* tends to reflect your state of mind or thoughts and emotions that are most prominent. For instance, if you're seething with anger at a person, it's likely that you'll receive a reading that comments on this anger, instead of the question itself.

2. Clarify. Create the perfect phrasing for the question. The *I Ching* only answers one question at a time. If you're looking for a forecast or prediction, you'll likely receive a muddled interpretation because the future is unknowable. *But* what you can do is prepare for the future and understand some aspect of life or writing with more clarity. Typically people create questions that ask for understanding or advice. For example you might ask: What approach should I take to this problem for the benefit of all involved? Or, What is the best way to understand the themes of my writing? Or, How can I work most effectively on this project? Or, what can I do to know my protagonist better?

3. Write down the question. I suggest that you designate a specific notebook as a record for each time you use *The Writer's I Ching* and write down all your questions and answers so that there is no confusion later. First, write down the question in your notebook. Next, pick up the deck and shuffle the cards while thinking about your question. You can evolve your own method for choosing a card, but one that works well is after shuffling the cards, divide the deck into three piles. Then, pick up the middle pile and place it on top and realign the deck. Flip over the top card which will reveal the hexagram with your answer.

Next, write down the number, the hexagram symbol, and main points of the answer. You might also want to review the combination of elements that make up the hexagram (wind, lake, thunder, etc.) and think about how these elements can contribute to your understanding. For example, perhaps the mountain reminds you of emotional and mental stability or you associate thunder as a harbinger of change, as when weather brings about change. Another suggestion is to place the card you've chosen in your office or work space as a reminder of your answer while you write.

Questions

The *I Ching* is helpful for many types of inquiry: achieving goals, making decisions, guiding personal interactions, and plotting your career path. Because it is based on a world of symbols, it can also reveal hidden forces in your unconscious that need to be brought to light. Its remarkable ability to describe the practical, emotional, and psychological conditions of your life is of immense value in knowing yourself. It brings you gently but firmly to profound realizations. These truths have a way of being both reassuring and challenging, and provide a foundation for personal growth and exploration.

It does not matter what type of goal you're aiming for, in your career, inner life, or relationships; you can use the wisdom of the *The Writer's I Ching* to create firm steps and strategies to achieve your goals. It can cast light on future possibilities because it offers a means of examining your options. It can help you step into the proper flow of things or adopt a positive mindset. There are so many ways that *The Writer's I Ching* can help writers plan their days and years.

Examples of questions are:

- How can I remain calm and focused while working on this project?
- Reveal the true image of myself at this time.
- What is my purpose in writing this (novel, story, essay)?
- What is the first step for achieving my goal?
- What is holding me back from achieving my goals?
- How can I overcome this obstacle or problem?'
- How will taking on this new job affect my writing schedule?
- What is the most productive time for my writing?

- Which project should I take on first?
- Which project deserves to be my main priority?

Time to begin

Your future is beckoning, enticing; the possibilities for your life and writing are endless. There are choices ahead, bridges to cross. But for this moment, come back to the now. Begin where you are in your life and open yourself to the wisdom gathered in these cards and in this book. And simply ask.

Six: The 64 Hexagrams

Every nightmare hints at the secret reserves
of imaginative power in the human mind.
What the stalled or not-yet-started writer needs
is some magic for getting in touch with himself, some key.
—John Gardner

The Hexagrams

The eight trigrams are made up of 64 combinations (8 x 8 = 64) of factors that create hexagrams, also called guas. Each offers profound inspiration, guidance, and information. Each hexagram or oracle is a symbol and is formed by paired energies, one over another, such as wind over water, which together create a new meaning. With this coming together, the power of natural forces operating in the world and within our own inner cosmos merge. Always remember that the *I Ching* is a means to talk to yourself and comprehend and work with the change that is always happening in the world. The symbols of each hexagram provide a language we can access and make us participants in our destiny rather than passive onlookers. The hexagrams speak to the duality within, and the forces, emotional states, doubts, and external affairs that influence us daily.

—

1. Creativity: Heaven/Heaven

We are cups, constantly and quietly being filled. The trick is,
knowing how to tip ourselves over and let the beautiful stuff out.
—Ray Bradbury

The heavens are infinite, brimming with stars, planets, and moons. The heavens are also an eternal source of inspiration, a reminder of the amazing creative potential in each of us. This is the first of eight hexagrams that doubles the primary elements. This hexagram depicts your limitless imagination and your capacity to initiate things. It also refers to the many ways you are energized and can create new beginnings, opportunities, and positive changes. The heavens act as a catalyst and a harbinger of success. Use this primal force now, especially if you need to feel rejuvenated or shake up the status quo.

In practical terms, it indicates a potent time to write, begin new projects, and act on ideas. It is also a reminder that creativity is a renewable resource. Realize what it brings to your life and use its force to push ahead. Remain true to your expression of self, beliefs, and story ideas. Remember that everything that happens under the stars can teach you and inspire you toward your next step.

While creativity is a powerful catalyst, you will not succeed unless it is linked to will and focus. If you've been delaying or hesitating about starting a project, this indicates a favorable time to set plans in motion. This hexagram also warns you to consolidate your efforts and not waste time or energy on worthless or unimportant pursuits. Go forward and you'll be rewarded.

Fiction Question:

Inspiration is only the starting point when writing fiction. Ideas are not enough; anchor them with solid techniques, including the structure and underpinnings of plot that are so necessary to tell an engrossing tale. Many seemingly invisible techniques come together to shape fiction. Work at uncovering these elements. Understand how scenes are structured, how scenes are based on a goal or mission, how in each scene the protagonist or another main character encounters opposition, and how each scene characterizes the players, provides information, and propels the action forward.

Write about a protagonist who fascinates you, and get to know him or her intimately. Know why your protagonist acts as he does, how he is shaped by his past, what he wants in the story, and what he fears most. Make certain that your main characters are proactive and don't merely react to their situations or problems.

As you write your drafts, keep studying the subtler techniques found in your favorite novels. Notice transition devices, pacing, and how chapters end. Notice how language creates a mood and how sensory elements are included. If you draw this hexagram when your story has snagged, be assured that you have the means to solve your plot problems. However, go back to your original concept and make certain that it has enough density and complications to sustain the storyline and there is a tangible forward thrust to every scene.

Nonfiction Question:

Your advice is simple: become lost in wonder. Nonfiction writers often create their essays or memoirs from the mind-set of pragmatism. Or they approach their subjects, including their own history, as researchers or social scientists. While solid information is always helpful in creating believable and entertaining nonfiction, so is an attitude of wonder.

As you go through life, and especially as you approach writing topics, see the world through the eyes of a child. Stop analyzing and start feeling and noticing. In *Becoming a Writer* Dorothea Brande wrote this advice:

> . . . (T)he author of genius does keep till his last breath the spontaneity, the ready sensitiveness, of a child, the "innocence of eye" that means so much to the painter, the ability to respond freshly and quickly to new scenes and to old scenes as though they were

new; to see traits and characteristics as though each were new-minted from the hand of God instead of sorting them quickly into dusty categories and pigeonholing them without wonder or surprise; to feel situations so immediately and keenly that the word "trite" has hardly any meaning for him; and always to see "the correspondence between things" of which Aristotle spoke two thousand years ago. This freshness of response is vital to the author's talent.

The Writer's Path:

You are infinitely creative and need to constantly feed the source of your inspirations and ideas. One method of nurturing inspiration is to use a writer's journal so that your ideas are not lost. This journal is unlike a diary because instead of looking inward, you are noticing, always noticing. Make note of the heavens and everything around you; a writer's first task is awareness. This habit of awareness will sift into your writing and will in turn bring about more inspiration.

Another reminder in this first hexagram is to trust in your ideas. In fact, be assured that writing is your destiny. You are a unique voice, and you can be heard. Do not be concerned with others' opinions. Listen instead to inner guidance and use your writing talents to benefit humankind.

—

2. Receptive: Earth/Earth

In all the major genres, vivid detail is the lifeblood of fiction...
If we carefully inspect our experiences as we read,
we discover that the importance of physical detail is that it creates for us
a kind of dream, a rich and vivid play in the mind.

Six: The 64 Hexagrams

We read a few words at the beginning of the book or the particular story, and
suddenly we find ourselves seeing not words on a page
but a train moving through Russia,
an old Italian crying, or a farmhouse battered by rain. We read on—
not passively but actively, worrying about the choices the characters have
to make, listening in panic for some sound behind the fictional door,
exalting in characters' successes, bemoaning their failures.
—John Gardner, The Art of Fiction

Earth over Earth suggests the solidity and vastness of the earth, its prairies, mountains, and deserts. The earth is immense and nourishing, and provides a home to many. This hexagram recommends that you remain open and receptive to change and inspiration. The earth also holds all, the good and bad, the overwhelming and gentle forces of nature. And like the earth, we learn to develop breadth, strength, and largesse.

Hexagram 2 describes achieving balance, staying grounded and stable. Being receptive does not mean that you abdicate responsibility or look to others for answers. This is not a time for confrontations or accusations. Instead, be willing to listen to people you respect, while remaining open to change and opportunity. Pay close attention to your intuition and the signs around you. Notice synchronicity. Be open to guidance. And be willing to work hard.

Fiction Question:

The fictional world must be a living, breathing entity in a story. Setting is not merely a backdrop or lifeless prop; it is your story's milieu and provides tone, mood, action, and motivation. Use the power of place to bring your story to vibrant life. Include weather, geography, nature, time of day, season, and natural lighting. Make sure that your buildings and interiors characterize the people who live in them.

Remember too that setting should make things happen. Fog obscures the crime scene, snow causes accidents, rain brings on gloom, and lightning storms cause power outages. Thus think of setting as an interactive force, especially one that creates mood.

If you are writing fantasy or science fiction, take time to build a remarkable, imaginative, and complete world so that the reader can easily enter this new reality. Make decisions about the level of technology in your story world, how the government works, its monetary system and military. Is your world a matrilineal or patriarchal society? Does it have four seasons? A sun and moon? Use fresh details so the reader understands all the aspects of your world, including its physical aspects, history, politics, religions, and culture.

Nonfiction Question:

A work of creative nonfiction must be grounded in the ordinary details of life in much the same way that fiction is. All writing requires that readers enter a world, a specific reality. Nonfiction is not abstract; it is not mere ideas or facts embroidered with a smattering of examples. For instance, if you want to write about injustice, or freedom, or liberalism, these broad concepts cannot be brought to life unless we see them affecting real people. The broader or more abstract the topic, the more necessary it is to nail it down with specific people acting in vivid ways that bring about the reader's understanding of the topic. If you're interested in writing personal essays or memoirs, it might be necessary to forget the techniques from your school years. When you wrote essays or reports for your teachers, it wasn't necessary to focus on people or to use narrative techniques. But the creative nonfiction written today is a meld of techniques; it borrows from other genres; and is concrete and brimming with sensory details and the artifacts of life. Write about people using narrative techniques such as scene structure, dialogue, and setting details whenever possible to provide a context for the issues you're illustrating. Nonfiction is about life, not concepts, and it often tells a story while weaving in themes or broader issues.

The Writer's Path:

The earth is ancient, and nature, while it exerts a relentless and sometimes destructive force, remains steady and constant. Be steady and anchor yourself solidly with compassion for yourself and others. Be receptive to new ideas and inspirations. Spend time alone and maintain an inner calm while you quietly eliminate distractions and worry. Your intuition is especially reliable right now. Trust your inner voice; it is sometimes more instructive than analytical or deductive reasoning. While it's helpful to listen to trusted advisors, their wisdom is most beneficial when you understand yourself deeply.

———

3. Uneven Beginning: Water/Thunder

For a true writer each book should be a new beginning where he tries again for something that is beyond attainment.

—Ernest Hemingway

The ancient Chinese represented this hexagram as a blade of grass pushing through the ground into the sunlight. The elements of water over thunder suggest beginnings and tremendous energy. Think of the uneven beginning as the turbulent stretch of river just before it reaches the waterfall and the mighty downward plunge. As the river tumbles over the falls, thunder erupts. The wild water always reaches the bottom, just as a seed inevitably transforms into a bloom and a child becomes an adult.

———

All things have a beginning, middle, and end. While the potential in the beginning of a new cycle or project can be impressive, sometimes there is also confusion, chaos, and darkness. There can also be giddiness, overexcitement, and feelings of being out of control. But from this struggle emerges order, beauty, and triumph.

Whether you're ready or not, a new cycle has begun. You cannot avoid it. Handle the newness with care and work through your confusion. A missed step or bad decision in the beginning can lead to problems later. Since traversing rapids is tricky and possibly dangerous, so this is a time to affiliate with others and seek guidance. Learn the lessons at this stage and remember what you've learned from the past. Walk carefully; dangers may appear, but can be overcome with guidance, patience, and perseverance.

Fiction Question:

Examine your opening pages and make certain that they sizzle or contain a quiet intensity that forces a reader to continue. The opening pages in fiction have a huge job to do. They must introduce characters, setting, voice, point of view, and the story question that is created by the *inciting incident*—the first major action that pushes the story forward and threatens or shakes up your protagonist's status quo. The action in the opening scene should rattle the protagonist, setting the stage for further complications, obstacles, and trials. It should also create sympathy for the protagonist and introduce his initial goal. Characters without goals or motivation are characters the reader cannot care about.

Often, the most compelling beginnings are created by plunging directly into the middle of events or *in medias res*. This powerful technique creates a hook and a focus for the opening scene. Thus, don't start with backstory; start with change, intrigue, and suggestions of upcoming conflict. Use setting and description judiciously, but make certain that your reader is instantly transported into your fictional world.

Nonfiction Question:

There are many techniques and style tricks that make for effective nonfiction. But to emulate them, you must first notice how published writers work their magic. Analyze and emulate the techniques of nonfiction masters.

Notice how great writers like Truman Capote, Joan Didion, or Gay Talese use narrative techniques and anecdotes to bring a story to life. Notice how dialogue sprinkled throughout nonfiction adds substance and action. Notice too style tricks such as alliteration and metaphor, how Norman Mailer and M.F.K. Fisher anchor their writing with sensory images and data. Notice how nonfiction writers adjust the voice to fit the subject matter—at times whimsical or sarcastic or droll. Read widely, including contemporary writers and greats from the past—Charles Kuralt, Mary Karr, Tobias Wolff, Adrienne Rich, Carlos Fuentes, James Baldwin, Richard Selzer, Scott Russell Sanders, Virginia Woolf, Mary McCarthy, H.L. Mencken, and James Thurber.

The Writer's Path:

No matter if you cannot see the way; simply begin. Trust that the act of writing contains its own power, and ideas will gradually emerge into the light and then solidify if you commit to them.

If you have selected this hexagram, consider beginning a project that has long intrigued you but that you've avoided because its complexity frightens or overwhelms you. Accept the fact that large or complicated projects can be daunting, and start anyway. Proceed thoughtfully, first organizing your material, then creating systems and outlines to help the process.

If you're feeling fretful or impatient, find ways to calm yourself. It's not a time to hurry. Instead, devise structures or a foundation to sustain your project.

It's never been a better time to be a writer, with so many books and re-sources available. Use them, especially during moments of confusion. Remember that the answers are out there.

Uneven Beginning reminds you also to never dwell on past mistakes or re-jections. This is a chance for a fresh start, so submit to the necessary learning curve and always look to the future.

———

4. Inexperience: Mountain/Water

Writing itself is one of the great, free human activities. There is scope for individuality, elation, and discovery. In writing, for the person who fol-lows with trust and forgiveness what occurs to him, the world remains always ready and deep, an inexhaustible environment, with the combined vividness of an actuality and flexibility of a dream. Working back and forth between experience and thought, writers have more than space and time can offer. They have the whole unexplored realm of human vision.

—William Stafford

The fourth hexagram is often interpreted as folly, but it stems from inex-perience, not stupidity. Early translations referred to this hexagram as childhood, and the elements of mountain over water portray a spring flowing out of a mountain.

While you might be competent in many areas of your life, you're facing a situation that might seem beyond your capabilities. You can use your youth-ful qualities to your benefit now if you can temper innocence and carefree attitudes.

Another way to look at the situation is to accept your limitations and work with them. Ask for help. Don't wait for a teacher or mentor to magically appear—seek him out. And once you have found him, use your time together wisely; absorb knowledge and advice. Ask questions, but don't keep asking the same questions because it will confuse the issue. Don't assume that you know more than you know. Humility is a valuable trait in a writer.

Don't skip important lessons. Confusion is sometimes part of life and part of writing. Patiently write your way out of the confusion.

Fiction Question:

Many beginning writers base their first manuscript on people, events, or experiences from real life. However, while fiction can borrow from life, it is much bigger, and more frightening, and the stakes are always higher. You see, fiction is artifice. If you are writing a story based on truth, you will need to alter it and pump it up somehow. There is another point that bears considering: fiction is held together by a structure that keeps it from meandering or veering into nonsense. Real life is full of random events and coincidences. Events in fiction are always causally related or connected. Robin Hemley offers this helpful explanation:

> Real life, if yours is anything like mine, tends towards chaos.
> Fiction has structure, order, refinement. Imposing the artificial—
> that's what fiction writers do to turn their stories into art. Fiction
> can be boisterous, even obnoxious at times. The art of writing fic-
> tion, like a good magic trick, is often in making it seem easy,
> effortless—in never letting the reader see all the practice you've
> put into it.

> The temptation, which must always be resisted, is to include
> *everything* that happened, rather than making wise selections. Be
> parsimonious with your experience. Don't give it added weight
> simply because you're fond of the memory. If you include every-

thing that happened, your book or story risks becoming muddled and weighted down by a voluminous chronicle of your associations. Remember, this is a piece of fiction, not a slide show of your various experiences.

Nonfiction Question:

The human heart is a vast, rich territory to be explored, as are the choices we all make in life and the transitions we progress through. To be human is to be part of a constantly swirling drama and mystery. People encounter loss as they live their lives, and this too is rich territory for writing. The best nonfiction tracks a writer on the road to discovery.

But one of the ways that nonfiction can go astray is when it is used for venting or therapy. Simply having pain is not a reason to write. Ask yourself why you're writing—to discover the truth, to leave a legacy, to remember, to understand what happened to you. No matter the reason, analysis is required. A good essay or memoir is reflective and honest, and arrives at some important truth. The subject always matters and the writer considers the reader at all times. And the facts of life are empty until you fill them with memory, craft, and imagination.

The Writer's Path:

The writing path is part childhood wonder, part artistry, part business. If you have selected this hexagram, consider how you can balance your love of writing with practical concerns. A writer has several personalities combined in one body. This isn't some troubling psychosis, but it means that while writing is a business, the artistry to create it comes from a deeper, more innocent source within.

Some *I Ching* texts call this hexagram the Happy Fool. But you need to question whether your lack of business savvy and practical experience is hampering your writing path. Are you a happy fool or simply a fool? Cherish your innocence and artist's soul, but also master solid skills and business practices.

———

5. Waiting: Water/Heaven

There is only one thing that you should do. Go into yourself.
Find out the reason that commands you to write; see whether it has spread
its roots into the very depths of your heart; confess to yourself
whether you would have to die if you were forbidden to write.
This most of all: ask yourself in the most silent hour of your night:
must I write? Dig into yourself for a deep answer. And if this answer rings
out in assent, if you meet this solemn question with a strong, simple "I must,"
then build your life in accordance with this necessity;
your whole life, even its humblest and most indifferent hour,
must become a sign and witness to this impulse.

—Rainer Maria Rilke

In this hexagram the ancient Chinese revealed their dependence on rainfall. In this agrarian country, rainfall was vital to all aspects of life. When translated into modern times and your daily life, Waiting refers to the need for patience.

The typical Western approach to careers and problems is to forge ahead, pedal to the metal. For centuries, Eastern philosophies have suggested gentler, slower, and more intuitive ways of operating in the world. This hexagram confirms that sometimes calculated or appropriate waiting, after stopping to determine exactly what the situation requires, works best.

In everyone's life there are lulls and plateaus, as when waiting for a storm to sweep through or dawn to arrive until you resume your normal activities. Appreciate these quieter times and adopt a mindset of steadiness and trust. Believe that the way will open eventually. Carry on as if all is well, conserving your strength.

Fiction Question:

Fiction is often based on revelations, secrets, or solving a mystery. The trick to working with these factors in a story is to make certain that information is revealed slowly and that you use delay tactics to create suspense and worry in the reader. Revelation comes in many forms. It can be the identity of the murderer, the essence of a character, or secrets from a character's past. But revelation is like a striptease act, and when properly handled the writer doles out bits of information in small increments, saving the most important revelations until the last possible moment. Delay also helps build tension and creates slowly rising conflict and involvement in the reader.

Thus, find ways to *delay* information, perhaps keeping the protagonist in the dark if appropriate or creating a series of missteps that delay uncovering the truth. As you develop the cast for your story, give the main characters a secret or perhaps an agenda that they're hiding so you have the layers of intrigue a story requires. It's also helpful to know how far a character will go to protect his reputation, secret, or motives. Remember too that secrets and revelations must matter to the story, must drive characters to act in certain ways.

Nonfiction Question:

Paying attention strengthens your senses and rewards you with detail and nuance that you can insert into your stories. Paying attention enriches your viewpoint with the interesting, the blemished, the grotesque—unusual people, objects, and events.

Awareness is also directly linked to your intuition. Thus it is necessary to nurture your intuition, remembering that often your inspirations arrive unbidden, catching you by surprise. Notice the timing of these whispers—do they happen when you are driving, showering, or walking? Once you notice *when* your insights arrive, start setting up the conditions to experience them again and again.

Then capture these insights by writing them down. Inspiration will wither over time if ignored. Recording these flashes of brilliance guarantees that they will happen more often. While you're at it, write down your dreams, trying to interpret the messages contained in these nighttime dramas. Creative people notice everything, but also spend time musing about what they see.

The Writer's Path:

If you are waiting for an editor or agent to respond, try not to fret. Stay busy instead. Don't dissipate valuable energy by worrying or being fearful. It's especially important to not overreact or strike back during this time.

If your writing has shortcomings, Waiting is a fertile period for correction and improvement. Keep editing and rewriting, but don't obsess about your shortcomings.

Other suggestions are to care for your body, nourish your mind, and remain calm and trusting. All writers should walk to counteract the effects of long hours spent sitting and to stimulate creativity and memory. Consider yoga or other means to strengthen the body and soothe the mind.

Trust in the power of destiny. If you live in trust and calm while producing and constantly improving, the universe will notice and reward you. Dreams take time.

6. Conflict: Heaven/Water

The three greatest rules of dramatic writing: Conflict! Conflict! Conflict!
—James N. Frey, *How to Write a Damn Good Novel*

In this hexagram, the overpowering aspects of heaven extending upward and the yin flow of water moving downward create conflict. Both heaven and water have limitless capacity and can thereby stir up trouble. Hexagram 6 warns that there is potential for huge drama and strife when conflict is present.

In fact, conflict is inevitable in everyone's life. To minimize the painful effects of conflict, first weigh all the outcomes and possibilities before you begin an endeavor. Anticipate problems before they occur, choose the more prudent path, and make certain that people around you understand your position. Tread carefully and deal with issues before they loom too large to resolve. If the conflict has already appeared, negotiate and meet your enemy or opponent halfway.

Fiction Question:

Conflict is the key to all fiction. While in real life you probably avoid situations that cause strife, your job as the creator of fiction is to create conflict for your characters at every turn.

But also consider subtler means to introduce tension and conflict. Whenever possible, create tension in the scene for your protagonist. Find small ways to make him squirm. If he's a smoker, place him in a setting where smoking is not allowed. If he abhors smoke, place him in a room as smoky as a Paris jazz club in the 1920s. Or, if he has a busy day, use weather to hinder his movements or cause misery—blinding rain, blizzards, relentless heat, sweltering humidity. Bestow headaches, colds, the strain of overwork, indigestion, and all sorts of physical discomforts in your scenes. Create traffic jams or car trouble when he's in a hurry to reach a destination. Embarrass and humiliate him; have him get caught rifling through another character's belongings. Your protagonist's discomfort creates tension, which in turn makes readers experience his emotions.

Nonfiction Question:

Every writer must develop a means of editing and rewriting, but sometimes it's helpful to keep a checklist or questions on hand with which to evaluate an early draft. Here are questions to use to evaluate a work of nonfiction:

- Does the beginning invite the reader into the story or essay and pique his interest? What is your emotional response to the writing?
- Is the writing creative and original?
- Is the writing style polished, consistent, and appropriate to the form?
- Is the writing mostly in the active voice, with vivid verbs and precise nouns?
- Is there a variety in sentence length and structure?
- Does the writer rely too often on modifiers and are there bland modifiers such as "very" and "quite" scattered on the pages?
- Are there any particular phrases, images, or scenes that stand out and linger?
- Were you confused by any aspect of the writing? Were there places where you needed more information?
- Is there enough or too much description?
- Does the dialogue work? Is there too much? Does it sound realistic?
- Does dialogue move the story forward, provide necessary information, or reveal the people depicted?

- Does the writer explain too much? (Julia had never been so angry in her life.)
- Is the piece organized clearly and succinctly?
- Does the ending deliver? That is, does it provide impact, conclude the theme, and linger in your imagination?

The Writer's Path:

Write no matter what dramas and conflicts are happening in your life. Storms will rage, lovers will leave, and friends will disagree. Write despite the weather, your broken heart, or bruised feelings. There will never be perfect conditions for writing, when all is peace and tranquility. Chances are, once one area of your life smoothes out, another will erupt. Find the equanimity within, no matter the conditions in your outer world.

---

7. The Army: Earth/Water

Nothing astonishes men so much as common sense and plain dealing.
—Ralph Waldo Emerson

This hexagram represents a dynamic, unstoppable force, such as a bubbling spring that rises from deep in the ground and reaches the surface with might and sweetness. Understand the laws of gravity and force and how the collective energy of people gathered together in a common cause creates might.

The Army also suggests that this is the time to be organized, disciplined, and focused on worthwhile projects. Think like a general with an eye on the big picture. Be indomitable, but not overbearing. War should always be your last resort. This hexagram reminds you that being methodical, committed, and far thinking brings success. If you have mis-stepped, it is time to regroup, rethink, and reorganize to make things right.

Tap into universal energy, remembering that the earth is fruitful. Prosperity is suggested here. Hone your strategies, and deal with everyone using fairness, justice, and discernment.

Fiction Question:

Scenes are the building blocks of fiction. They happen in the now, create movement, and cause readers to be involved and worried. Each scene must be staged in a distinct time and place and populated with sharply defined characters, preferably with the protagonist facing opposition or a force. One of the simplest structures for shaping scenes is to remember that most scenes involve the protagonist wanting something—a scene goal—and someone or something prevents him from achieving it. Knowing this simple structure, you can create scenes based on conflict.

Consider creating scene cards to track your story and help stage it. A scene card contains details such as:

- Location:
- Time:
- Day:
- Weather:
- Cast:
- Opposition/conflict:
- Action:
- Scene Goal:
- Failure or success:

Nonfiction Question:

Explore universal themes and write for the good of humankind. Too often memoirists and nonfiction writers write for themselves, to make sense of their lives, or to reminisce. But the reader comes first, and this is an especially auspicious time to tap into the concerns of society. Yes, tell your story, but consider the larger issues and the essential questions of what it means to be a man or woman living in these times.

When examining your life or mining the past, ask yourself what it all means.

Often, we understand ourselves, our families, and significant events after a long period of time has passed. Or we spend our lives puzzling, teasing out the meaning of things, then fail to connect our personal insights to larger issues.

Marilyn Ferguson, the author and poet, suggests, "In most lives insight has been accidental. We wait for it as primitive man awaited lightning for a fire. But making mental connections is our most crucial learning tool, the essence of human intelligence; to forge links; to go beyond the given; to see patterns, relationship, context."

The Writer's Path:

In a word: affiliate. Join the hive; become part of a working group of writers. During this process, define your goals and interests, considering how your work adds to the greater good of all. If you are able, define and refine your goals now, keeping in mind your gifts to the world. The Army reminds you that when the time is right, the collective power and help of others will back your aims.

Another suggestion from The Army is to prove that you're a team player, especially when dealing with editors and agents. Show that you're trustworthy and professional in all your dealings. Deliver on time, keep your promises, and park your ego at the door. Finally, be supportive and generous to fellow writers, but don't dissipate your energy by spending more time critiquing and advising others than you spend on your own craft.

———

8. Unity: Water/Earth

The universe is made of stories, not of atoms.

—Muriel Rukeyser

The yin energy of water above is supported by solid ground. Water flows to fill in the emptiness of earth. This hexagram speaks most deeply about community, cooperation, connection, and responsibility to the group. Enhance your life by your connections to others and work together for important causes. If you have leadership qualities, this is the time to use them for the betterment of all.

The Unity hexagram also suggests that you are in the midst of a stressful time. Relationships might be ending and things might be changing around you, and you're struggling to understand what these changes mean. Accept change and get rid of old ideas. If you look closer, you'll notice that there is underlying support from another person or your community. Move toward harmony and take on responsibility if it's called for.

Fiction Question:

When readers first meet the protagonist in a story, they see him reacting to a change in his world because of the inciting incident. This event, a troubling change in the status quo, causes stress, forces the character to make a decision, and choose a goal. However, this initial goal often doesn't last the entire story or is resolved in the first scenes. Thus, you'll be creating a series of changes to inflict on your characters and these changes will in turn cause them to create more goals and plans.

This means the inciting incident is only the opening volley in a larger battlefield. As you plot, make certain that your characters, particularly the protagonist, become increasingly involved in the story's events, which in turn keep thrusting him into new decisions and directions. His motivation and resolve deepen as events push him closer to the antagonist, solving the problem, or self-discovery. Increasing motivation is also linked to increasing stakes and dangers as the story progresses. And these factors all add to satisfying drama.

Nonfiction Question:

Write about your faith or your beliefs about some important aspect of life. Taoist philosophy describes belief as unseen trust that carries and supports you in becoming who you are meant to be. In his Letter to the Hebrews, St. Paul describes faith as "the substance of things hoped for, the evidence of things unseen."

The topic of faith and belief is a complicated one, because people often assume it relates strictly to religion. But faith or belief is certainly not confined to religious or spiritual matters. You can believe in a person, a lifestyle, or the power of laughter.

The Writer's Path:

Sometimes writers wrongly believe that the writing life is a monastic one. But nothing can be further from the truth. It's vital that you balance your many hours alone with time spent among people, gathering inspiration to fill your creative reservoirs. See yourself as part of your community, not separate from it. Be aware of the issues of the day and think about them as a person with a large heart. There are times to be alone, but this is not one of them. Reach out and connect.

—

9. Restraint: Wind/Heaven

Simplify! Simplify! Simplify!

—E.B. White

Restraint describes the taming power of small forces. It comes from two Chinese characters, the first meaning little and the second meaning raising livestock or storing something. The second character can also refer to nourishment or conserving strength. The structure of the hexagram, wind over heaven, shows how clouds sometimes form in the sky, yet don't bring rain. Heaven has more yang energy than wind, so it temporarily restrains matters from progress or forward motion.

When your energy is depleted, gather your strength instead of forging ahead. Take a break. There is a possibility of eventual success, but your time will be best spent making plans and preparations, refining your vision. Don't act; instead, attempt gentle persuasion. Although you are advised to wait or approach other people with patience and tact, aspects are still favorable. You might also be chosen to show restraint within a group or subdue a plan or action that has gotten out of hand.

To achieve your goals now you need to remain firmly determined within, while your outward manner is gentle and adaptable. If you prepare properly, when the rain finally falls you'll be ready for it.

Fiction Question:

Subtlety is a word that writers rarely use when describing or discussing fiction. Yet sometimes when a story falters, it might be what is needed on all levels: in diction, style, sentence structure, and voice. A lack of subtlety in larger fictional elements also leads to bizarre or unbelievable characters, scenes that are overblown or wander, and subplots that take off like a cattle stampede.

We live in a multimedia society that dazzles us with sophisticated technology: web sites that leap off the screen with snappy graphics, movies enhanced by computerized wizardry, and gadgets that allow us to be plugged in 24/7. Amid this cacophony, we tend to overwrite or give in to gimmickry. But this can result in gaudiness in a story, and in the end our fictional world becomes weird and false.

So before you overdo and shout at readers with your strained efforts, remember what the reader brings to your pages. He is your partner in this enterprise and brings his memories, sensibilities, and understanding of human nature. And your reader wants you to trust him. Subtlety is a fine art when applied to fiction, and well worth the effort.

Nonfiction Question:

Revelation can sometimes be a two-edged sword in creative nonfiction. On the one hand, much of the intrigue in nonfiction stems from the reader's need to know, to learn intimacies and secrets, and to witness the writer's mind at work.

On the other hand, revealing parts of your life is sometimes unnecessary or in bad taste. Or it may injure the people you are writing about. Since this hexagram recommends tact, a nonfiction writer must ask himself difficult questions before writing about certain events. Will there be fallout from my revelations? Will my words humiliate someone? Will this incident make my reader uncomfortable?

Take the long view at this time. While the short-term payoffs might seem attractive, you need to write with your legacy in mind. Self-restraint will benefit your image in the end.

The Writer's Path:

Some writers can work amid chaos, but most cannot. If you step into your office and your desk is buried under a blizzard of papers and your filing system is nonexistent, you'll be less effective during your writing sessions. The hexagram Restraint suggests that you conquer the small parts of your life and manage the details in your day-to-day existence. Tame your environment, especially your workspace. Create systems to manage paperwork, files, and information. Once you have created systems, keep them up to date.

This is also a good time for research and editing. All writers need to research their topics to make them authentic. Research is a foundation for writing and creates confidence. However, beware of researching, busywork, and surfing the Internet instead of actually writing and rewriting. If you're in the midst of rewriting, don't make drastic changes, but concentrate on polishing the language.

10. Caution: Heaven/Lake

Nothing leads so straight to futility
as literary ambitions without systematic knowledge.

—H.G. Wells

The powerful yang forces of heaven swirl above yin waters below. In this struggle the lake resists being overpowered. It signifies the strong treading on the weak, but not causing harm. In your life you might feel inspired and creative, but the outcome of an issue will be determined by how you conduct yourself. The oracle suggests using gentle means, caution, and care.

Be dignified in all your dealings, no matter the circumstances. Be especially tactful and diplomatic when coping with difficult people. If you're criticized by your fellow writers or an editor, swallow your irritation and don't retaliate. Don't cower either, but proceed carefully.

This is also a good time to face whatever frightens you, and to be prepared when facing dangers. Avoid committing to too many projects at once. Prioritize. Be alert and centered, but don't worry; conditions are favorable. Once you pass through this phase the results can be profound.

Fiction Question:

Beginning novelists are prone to overreach. They spin plots that are beyond their capabilities; they create complicated characters that the reader never comes to know intimately; they weave in too many subplots and themes that can drown out the story. Sometimes the story line zigzags back and forth in time at a dizzying pace. While ambition is always laudable, be practical when envisioning your first novel. Write a story that reflects your skill level.

Start with a protagonist whom you can come to know with the kind of intimacy reserved for selecting a marriage partner. Give this person an interesting dilemma, and then imagine the worst consequences of this dilemma, and how you complicate his life while the situation plays out. Based on your character's predicament, give him goals, but make achieving these goals difficult. Imagine a world that is textured and real; add a few supporting characters with whom your protagonist can interact, thus showing various aspect of his personality. But keep it simple, within the bounds of your abilities.

Nonfiction Question:

Good writing is lean and unpretentious. It isn't dumbed down, but instead is crafted with elegance and simplicity. Too often sentences are cluttered with modifiers and prepositional phrases that drain the meaning from the noun and verb. Nouns and verbs are the building blocks of writing and must be respectfully given their due in each sentence.

Your first draft does not need to be well written or lean; it merely needs to land on the page so that you can edit and prune it into shape. As you begin trimming your sentences, take Gary Provost's advice and make certain that every word in every sentence has a job to do. If not, get rid of it.

While you prune, keep in mind that less is more. William Follett explains: "To eliminate wordiness is to insure emphasis. Whenever we can make 25 words do the work of 50, by reducing the span of attention required, we increase the force of thought."

The Writer's Path:

No matter if you're unpublished or have just signed a four-book contract, people skills are called for. While difficult people exist in all professions, it's dangerous to assume that the publishing world is filled with corruption and enemies. So avoid an adversarial outlook and don't act the part of the moody artist.

There is also risk in overreacting to or rejecting feedback or an editor's suggestions. No matter how stung you feel, react with poise. If there is a misunderstanding, work carefully to resolve it.

Treat editors and other professionals with courtesy, thoughtfulness, and respect. Send thank-you notes and follow your editor's guidelines about how, how often, and when to contact him or her. Act like a pro and you'll be treated like one.

———

11. Harmony: Earth/Heaven

It is not often that someone comes along who is a true friend
and a good writer.

—E.B. White, *Charlotte's Web*

The eleventh hexagram suggests the miracles of early spring. A period of growth, ease and prosperity is ahead and your writing projects will thrive. Enjoy your accomplishments, but also build a firm foundation for further successes. This is a good time to network and clear out the old to make way for the new.

During springtime, when the new buds burst out of the ground, the gardener must thin the new sprouts to avoid crowding. In this same way, you must eliminate the projects and habits that crowd out your writing. This pruning will make way for what is truly important, but it must be done with care. If negotiations are in progress, remain firm, focused, and fair. This is a good time for networking and taking advantage of new opportunities. When things are going well, don't become complacent. Keep moving toward your future, and triumph is assured.

Fiction Question:

Two work habits separate fiction writers: those who outline and those who do not. A fiction outline is quite different from those you learned in grade school. Those models of order, with Roman numerals, numbers, and letters, were a misery to construct. Designed to organize a topic, they seemed as creative as a straitjacket. So when you design a fiction outline, discard this model and invent an approach that fits your needs.

Some authors claim that they discover the story as they write it, but this writing-as-discovery method only works for some. Most writers work best by planning what is to come, or at least knowing the ending as they write. Just as you would not embark on a cross-country trip without a map, you cannot write a long manuscript without a plan. After all, how successful would your trip be if you stopped at every crossroad to guess which highway to take next? Your outline can be a modest paragraph that delineates your main character, his dilemma, obstacles to his success, and the outcome. Or you can create a chapter-by-chapter blueprint to follow. It's up to you, but don't set off on your fictional journey without knowledge of the terrain ahead.

Nonfiction Question:

Memoir writers need a deep understanding of narrative techniques. Without this understanding, your life story is doomed to flatness and mere reportage. Two terrific examples are found in *Don't Let's Go to the Dogs Tonight* by Alexandra Fuller and *This Boy's Life* by Tobias Wolff. Both are crafted with a novelist's techniques: scenes, cliffhangers, setting, sensory details, characterization, and dialogue. Both memoirs show people in peril and sizzle with tension.

Another technique to add to your repertoire is fictional structure. Learn how plot points work, how to create a hook, how to introduce conflict as the engine for storytelling, and how to create a climax that is emotionally satisfying. Read books on fiction technique and study how fiction writers weave their magic. One of the best primers for all writers is John Gardner's classic *The Art of Fiction*.

The Writer's Path:

The wisdom found in the *I Ching* often advises focus. Yet we question whether sages living centuries ago could have imagined the complicated and harried existence of the twenty-first century. For most of us, our days are crammed with obligations, tasks, and the demands of technology, work, and family.

But in the midst of this bedlam we must find an oasis of calm and quiet. And in this oasis, we must settle in and write. And then write some more. If you haven't created a schedule to achieve your writing goals, now is the time. If possible, write during your peak hours—the times when you are most energized and clearheaded. No matter if this means you'll be waking an hour earlier or going to bed an hour later. A sacrifice is likely called for; make it with the end in mind. As you write, focus on a single project to the exclusion of all others. Choose wisely and you'll succeed.

12. Standstill: Heaven/Earth

Being a writer is like having homework every night for the rest of your life.

—Lawrence Kasdan

In this hexagram, the yang energy of heaven and the softer yin energy of earth are at odds and seem unable to find common ground. Even though this situation appears difficult, it portrays wisdom that sheds light into the darkest corners. Standstill also suggests that practicing denial and self-control will be particularly beneficial now. This is especially true if you suffer from addictions or destructive habits. And because writing can cause stress and worry, addictions or self-medication can easily become a means of coping.

Doubts might be creeping in, or your lack of progress might worry you. If you're stuck or facing opposition, you need to back away from the source of trouble and use subtler approaches. If you ask for help, it will likely backfire. With that in mind, be wary of joining groups or asking for advice. Avoid negative people during this period; their presence will likely cause more harm than good. Since this is a difficult time, use it wisely and don't despair. If you're meant to be alone during this phase, so be it.

Fiction Question:

Dramatic structure is crafted in three acts and in the final act the climax delivers the strongest emotions. A scene is usually inserted shortly before the climax: the moment when your character faces the Dark Night of the Soul. In these lonely moments, he is faced with danger, a difficult decision, and few options for escape. Often, he has hit bottom and his worst flaw, such as pride or a hot temper, has proven to be his downfall. Sometimes he questions if it all has been worth the price he has paid or is about to pay.

An illustration of this moment is found in the movie version of *The Wizard of Oz*. The flying monkeys have whisked Dorothy away to the witch's castle. The witch, boiling with rage and impatient to wrest the ruby slippers from Dorothy, has imprisoned her in a room in an impenetrable tower. She leaves the room after overturning an hourglass on which tick away the final minutes of Dorothy's short life. All Dorothy's doubts and terrors surface and she finds herself longing for the safety of the farm in Kansas and her Auntie Em. She realizes how foolish she has been to leave that haven.

As she calls out, Em appears in the crystal ball, wearing her apron, her voice taut and her face etched with worry. Then the witch's frightening visage replaces it in the ball, mocking her in a hideous voice, "Auntie Em! Auntie Em!" A Dark Night of the Soul indeed. If your story structure, particularly when writing genre fiction, doesn't contain one, plan for this terrible struggle in which the character faces his worst fears and inner demons.

Nonfiction Question:

Often, the best nonfiction comes from the darkest corners of your soul. These emotionally intense experiences, the moments when you are bereft, ground down, humiliated, or terrified, supply the grist for writing nonfiction.

So where do these Dark Night of the Soul moments lie? The easiest answer is in the times when you thought you would not survive. People leave or die. You experience abandonment and trauma. You're fired, left behind, passed over, or rejected. A divorce devastates and shreds your dignity. Perhaps you discovered a poisonous family secret: that your teenager was using drugs, or your spouse was cheating on you. Maybe you were diagnosed with cancer, or your dreams were somehow dashed.

It is in these moments when you long to break down and surrender to despair that you are most tested. These tests are inherently dramatic, speak to the power of the human spirit, and reveal your strength, dignity, and courage. Perhaps you longed for these qualities, but could not muster them in the face of your pain.

Writers often approach these moments in one of two ways: denial or overexposure. This is a reminder to find a middle ground where you can reveal what needs to be revealed without wallowing in misery, pointing fingers, or portraying yourself as a victim. No matter how you reacted at the time, try to recall events from a distance with compassion for yourself while adhering to the truth.

The Writer's Path:

At times it is necessary to retreat or isolate yourself to get the work at hand done. If it's possible, leave home and find a place where you can work quietly without distractions. If it's not possible to escape, then sequester yourself with your computer and your project. No matter the season, cut back on social obligations, volunteering, and busywork. It is a time for being alone.

It is also a time to negotiate with your family in order to clear out responsibilities that steal time from your writing schedule. Pay a teenager to take over some tasks, bribe a partner, or leave others to shoulder your responsibilities. It is likely that you'll meet resistance to your plans, but hold your ground. It is vital that the people around you understand how important your writing is, no matter how they protest or try to distract you.

If your writing project is floundering now, don't despair. It is possible that you feel blocked or your progress is slow. Learn how to patiently work through these difficult times and you will discover what it truly means to be a writer.

---

13. Cooperation: Heaven/Fire

No matter what your level of experience, it is always an act of real trust to put new work out before other writers, live and in person. You feel rather like you've unwrapped your newborn and lain him down in the middle of people

who just happen to have rocks in their hands.

—Elizabeth Berg, *Escaping Into the Open: The Art of Writing True*

The intense and creative force of heaven rests above the fire burning below. When two passionate yang forces join together, the results can benefit both parties. The advice here also applies to business partnerships and writing groups. Work with purpose and send your creation into the marketplace. There is a powerful life force at the center of things. You can tap into it and become part of it.

Find common ground with like-minded writers. If a partnership or an anthology opportunity appears, plunge ahead. If there is an editor or agent whom you've been meaning to approach, now is the time. Joint efforts of any kind will work out. However, in the midst of a joint effort, it's important that the project, not an individual's agenda, is put first. Choose a role that best fits your abilities. On the other hand, if the project falters, be assured that answers and cooperation for the good of all are also possible. It's a time to reach out.

Fiction Question:

Fiction requires a cast of characters. This ensemble of neighbors, friends, coworkers, and enemies assures the reader that your fictional world is brimming with life just like the one he lives in. Yet this doesn't mean that you create a crowd merely for the sake of populating your story world. In fact, too many characters, especially in the opening scenes, can confuse the reader. Each time a reader meets a new character he must make room for him or her in his imagination. And if you keep adding to your cast, you can strain the reader's ability to recall everyone in your story. A crowded cast also makes it difficult for you to bestow each character with a distinct personality, purpose, and appearance.

Fabricate characters that who serve a distinct purpose in your story and enter the story world with their own agendas, quirks, and sparkle. Your villains must impress the reader with depth and purpose. Create characters designed to reveal the protagonist. If your character, an amateur detective, needs a sounding board, then she needs a friend or comrade to discuss the case with.

If you have created an introspective, unorthodox, sensitive, and complicated detective, such as P. D. James' Detective Inspector Adam Dalgliesh, then you need other characters to help reveal his personality. Since at times it appears that Dalgliesh is a bundle of contradictions, these relationships allow the reader insights into his inner workings. He is an accomplished poet and is often solitary. His poems and his aloofness are commented on by his fellow Scotland Yard employees and other characters. In the course of the series we learn that his wife died in childbirth and his missteps with relationships reveal how difficult it is for him to overcome his grief. For example, Kate Miskin works with Dalgliesh and they have a brief romantic relationship that doesn't last, illustrating the tenacity of his grief. Conrad Ackroyd is a long-time friend, so at times conversations with Ackroyd provide insights into the case, but also into the detective trying to solve it. There is also Emma Lavenham, a lecturer at Cambridge University and the woman who finally helps him commit to love again. Thus, members of your supporting cast have many purposes in a story, and are used to mirror your protagonist's personality, values, and beliefs, and also reveal his or her backstory.

Nonfiction Question:

Nonfiction is about people. True, themes are woven into our essays and memoirs, and we sometimes write about nature, pets, or travel. But life is lived among people who delight, intrigue, and sometimes annoy us, and among these people our stories lie. So explore relationships past and present because this is fertile ground to dig in. While exploring relationships, troubled or heavenly, keep asking yourself what this person means to you. And then go deeper, creating the whole person.

For example, it's easy to write about your grandparents, recalling the smells of a busy kitchen at holiday time. Perhaps you've brought your grandparents to life by describing them and recalling details of their home, or how they emigrated from Hungary. But your grandparents (or anyone you write about) cannot exist merely in relationship to you. See them the way a biographer or documentary filmmaker would see them: as people with childhoods, family influences, interests, politics, and standing in their communities or neighborhoods. See the whole person, not the one you view through sticky sentiment or childhood nostalgia.

The Writer's Path:

At some point, you will probably work with another person or a group on a project. This might mean working with an editor, an agent, or people in a critique group. Hexagram 13 reminds you that people can help you hone your writing skills or vision.

Collaborations, anthologies, or joint projects bring special rewards, yet can also foster difficulties and disagreements. Approach these collaborations with fairness, faith, and an open mind. Talk things over before you commit, and if necessary ask for the details in writing. If issues or problems arise, negotiate in good faith and always place the project before your own interests.

---

14. Great Harvest: Fire/Heaven

I began to write because I was too shy to talk, and too lonely not to send messages.

—Heather McHugh

The power of fire over the heaven's creative energies brings success and abundance. Take charge of your life and anything is possible. There are times for juggling various projects, but this is not such a time. Your situation calls for extreme focus and important choices about where to commit your time. Evaluate your priorities and upcoming projects with a careful eye. If you can concentrate on a single goal, success will follow.

Enjoy the rewards that come because terrific possibilities lie ahead. Arrange your schedule and shift your habits to take advantage of this time of potential and opportunity. A good support system is also indicated in this hexagram. Along with concentrating on your goal, eliminate negative emotions and keep your ego in check. Be realistic in all things, including your attitudes and values. This is an extremely fortunate period, so take advantage.

Fiction Question:

Theme, a central and unifying concept, underlies fiction. It is the idea behind the story. Theme reveals what it means to be human and how the world works. The way writers arrive at themes varies with the individual. Some writers begin a story or novel with a specific theme in mind, such as "greed" in Michael Crichton's *Jurassic Park*. Other common themes are betrayal, corruption, guilt, honor, vengeance, or intolerance. Others craft a story based on an intriguing character, dilemma, or idea, and then as they write, themes begin to emerge. Whatever method you choose, you are now reminded that theme is a solid underpinning.

Without theme, as without a structure, a story meanders and diverges into tangents; the reader does not arrive at insights about human nature. But if a writer keeps returning to his theme, especially when he is stuck or while editing, the story remains coherent and focused. In the best fiction, the themes are not heavy-handed or shrill; instead they whisper about the meaning of life and the price we pay for our humanity.

Nonfiction Question:

Sometimes when you are writing nonfiction, passion goes awry and your writing turns into a soapbox. The advice in this hexagram is to not preach; instead, trust your reader and allow him to read between the lines. The best nonfiction tells a story and points out truths without belaboring themes or bludgeoning the reader.

The deeper issue to keep in mind is that you don't own the truth. Tell the truth as you know it and allow the reader to draw his or her conclusions about the validity of your view.

The message in Great Harvest also urges you not to take yourself too seriously, and especially to work through negative emotions before they show up in your pages.

The Writer's Path:

Great Harvest assures you that your potential is enormous and your ideas are powerful. In order to gather the harvest, you need to work through emotions or moods that are hampering you. A professional writer is someone who has learned to work despite low spirits, poverty, or doubts. Into everyone's life some rain will fall, so the trick is to keep going when you get a little wet.

In careers such as dentistry or law, the professional will show up for work even if he is not in the mood. Somehow writers wrongly assume that they are exempt from this sort of work ethic. If their mood falters, so does their work.

So write despite your moods, your gloom, and your faltering spirit. You'll likely discover that when you work through these times, the work itself will dissipate them. Onward.

—

15. Modesty: Earth/Mountain

Quiet men with dreams can be dangerous.

—Colin Harrison, *The Havana Room*

This hexagram has a quieting quality and is symbolized by the stillness of mountains and the deep, stable force found within the earth. Modesty is a special hexagram because it signifies great fortune, and also reveals that humility was a highly valued attribute in long-ago China.

Translating this hexagram to your circumstance suggests that moderation creates balance and balance creates success. Thus, humility and perhaps silence are called for now. No matter the circumstances or difficulty, act and react with poise and reserve. Don't flaunt your successes; nor should you undervalue yourself and your time. This is also a reminder to remain realistic and quietly powerful.

Balance your writing craft; correct your habits of excess. Less is more. While editing, pay attention to the fundamentals and strive for simplicity, which in turn brings elegance.

Fiction Question:

—

Noah Lukeman's *The First Five Pages* describes the mistakes that doom a manuscript to rejection. Lukeman, a literary agent, has listed the errors writers make in order of importance. His first chapter deals with practical matters—the presentation of your manuscript to an agent. His second chapter, titled "Adjectives and Adverbs," discusses how the overuse of modifiers is the first problem that an agent or editor will notice in your pages. This habit is often the chief reason that writers are considered amateurs.

If you think that this sounds simplistic or harsh, think again. Excess modifiers will smother your sentences, your ideas, and your story. It takes only a few sentences or paragraphs before an editor realizes that your story is glutted with excess. Lukeman writes:

> Most people who come to writing for the first time think they bring their nouns and verbs to life by piling on adjectives and adverbs, that by describing a day as being "hot, dry, bright and dusty" they make it more vivid. Almost always the opposite is true.

While you're analyzing your modifiers, notice if you're using adverbs. They are seldom necessary, especially those that end in "-ly" such as quickly as in "walk quickly," and they repeat verbs, prop up weak verbs, or dilute strong verbs. A simple exercise is to print out your manuscript and go through it, highlighting every modifier. Try highlighting all your adverbs in blue and adjectives in yellow. If your pages are bruised with color, you're suffering from modifier overload and must trim, tighten, and reconsider each one.

Nonfiction Question:

Simple words are best. Bruce Ross-Larson writes in *Edit Yourself*: "Just as your speech is filled with many words that add nothing to what you say, your writing is often larded with words that obscure your meaning rather than clarify it. Trim this fat to direct your reader's attention to important words and ideas."

Write to communicate, not impress. Begin by questioning your superfluous modifiers, and mistrust words that are multi-syllabic and overblown. Also avoid jargon, acronyms, and abstractions. The best writing is grounded, concrete, and sensory.

Next, examine your nouns and verbs, the workhorses in your sentences. Choose them for their vibrancy and precision, and how they work together in a sentence. Verbs anchor stories, drive characters to prove their motivations, and create a world that breathes.

You can write, "The wind moved the birch leaves." Or, "The wind whispered through the birch trees, like a sigh settling over the lake." You can write, "The hurricane destroyed the town." Or, "The hurricane tore through the town, leaving a path of destruction." It's your choice.

The Writer's Path:

This hexagram advises moderation, modesty, and balance. It also reminds you to notice the seasons and rhythms in all things, and to pay attention to timing. Use your writing routine as a means to center yourself. If you write at the same time day after day with a quiet mind and genuine purpose, magic will happen. A writing routine is calming and balancing. It signals the subconscious that it is time for creativity, and this routine will make it easier for the words to come forth.

The warning now is to avoid extremes. No matter how great your need to overreact or dramatize a situation, rein in your inner drama queen. Regardless of your circumstances, remain humble, factual, and alert.

—

16. Thinking Ahead: Thunder/Earth

Pay attention to what they tell you to forget.

—Muriel Rukeyser

It's as if the intense power of thunder is calling to the quiet earth below. Yet even though thunder is rumbling overhead, this is still a period of harmony and ease. Because you've evaluated each situation carefully and done the hard work, you can reap the rewards. You can also give the green light to projects and jump in with enthusiasm. Then the seeds you have planted and your preparations from the past can be harvested.

This hexagram recommends establishing a firm foundation for your work. Such a foundation can be made up of many things—supportive friends and family, a comfortable workspace, a writing routine, an agent you can count on to negotiate for you and help plan your career. Employ management skills and think ahead, envisioning your career in the coming years. Build the foundation now and some day you'll be rejoicing over your publishing credits.

This is an ideal time to send your manuscript to an agent or editor. It also suggests that you keep amassing stories and projects so that if you do connect with a publishing professional, you'll be ready to submit your work.

Fiction Question:

In every culture, stories, myths, and fables are passed from generation to generation. In these stories we find archetypes or blueprints for themes and images that communicate the truth about human nature. Knowledge of archetypes can help push a writer deeper into his story, define character traits, and advance the plot trajectory.

Archetypes are found in ancient stories such as *The Odyssey*, and many modern novels and films such as *The Great Gatsby* and *Star Wars*. Carl Jung described archetypes as those "forms or riverbeds along which the current of psychic life has always flowed." He theorized that people share a collective unconscious, or "deposits of the constantly repeated experiences of humanity... a kind of readiness to reproduce over and over again the same or similar mythical ideas..." According to Jung, this common memory creates an understanding of certain archetypes that resonate and transcend culture.

A protagonist's nature will always reflect an archetype, which will be expressed in his dominant traits and actions. You can also use archetypes for creating secondary characters. A list of archetypes to consider when crafting characters: jester, innocent, femme fatale, sage, explorer, magician, outlaw, everyman, lover, ruler, creator, caregiver, Amazon, scorned lover, matriarch, betrayer, traitor, warrior/gladiator, derelict, fool, messiah, artist, abuser, warlock, best friend, rival, and lost soul.

Nonfiction Question:

Tone is the word that refers to the writer's attitude toward the subject, and can vary widely from witty to somber. Mitchell Ivers, a former editor at Random House, explains that three common mistaken tones are out-of-place humor, excessive formality, and misdirected anger. He writes:

> There are times when formality, humor and anger are appropriate, but all three are easy to slip into unintentionally. Writing with purpose is the best way to avoid inappropriate tone. If your purpose is to persuade, you will quickly realize that anger, condescension or sarcasm will not accomplish that goal.

Formality often creeps into a writer's voice because he is accustomed to writing term papers, school reports, or office memos. Jargon and formality work in a technical manual, but when a person writes essays or literary nonfiction, formality makes him appear insecure about his credibility. Formality is linked with seriousness of purpose only.

Humor also comes with risks, because it is so subjective and easy to overdo. Too many jokes and the writer comes off as being coy or silly. Too much sarcasm, exaggeration, or irony can wear on the reader.

Anger, even if it is justified, is perhaps the most difficult emotion to bring onto the page. Ivers explains that anger, even when deeply felt, is rarely persuasive, while reason combined with passion almost always is. Anger can alienate people and get in the way of communicating, so cool off before you approach a touchy subject.

The Writer's Path:

Your intuition is an amazing inner guidance system, but often its signals become jammed. Or it's too easy to ignore. But that small whispering voice, information that appears in dreams, or sudden flashes of insight, have enormous power to guide you.

Your first step in working with your intuition is to pay more attention to it. If you continually ignore this knowledge, the whisper is silenced over time. And you're left in an ordinary reality, without benefit of the source of wisdom that is your heritage.

You are imbued with this inner voice for a reason. Follow it. Notice what you're doing when it arrives and, if necessary, repeat these actions to invite it to return. Then write down your flashes of insight, your dreams, and your wonderings. There is power in the quietest of voices.

——

17. Flexibility: Lake/Thunder

Under the best circumstances, the process of writing
allows one to give oneself over to the imagination, trusting that within it,
we act in one's best interest,
trusting that the use of the creative, the descent in language into the self,
the rigorous scrutiny of the psyche, the inclination to dare the unknown
will seriously enhance one's life. . . . .
Sometimes the simple willingness to explore one's life story asserts the reality
of the individual, which is otherwise so often undermined.

And as it is almost impossible to disentangle or distinguish the process of writing from one's development as a person, this, in itself, is the beginning of healing.

—Deena Metzger

You are heading toward a breakthrough. If you step into the flow of energy, new possibilities will appear. There are layers of meaning in Flexibility, but there are two main concepts to focus on. The first suggests following your conscience in decisions that are at hand. Make choices based on impeccable standards and integrity.

The second recommends adopting a practical mind-set for dealing with your writing projects. It might be necessary to abandon something that is not working to make way for a project or situation that will bring success. Don't waste time on old paths; widen your approach and outlook. If you can keep an open mind, you'll likely learn an important lesson.

Fiction Question:

One of the most difficult decisions every writer faces is when to pull the plug on a project that is floundering. There are projects that are publishable, and unfortunately, some projects that will never be published. No matter how we struggle and rewrite, some simply never jell.

The reasons for these failings are many: characters who don't come to life; a plot that never quite takes off; clichéd writing or plotting; conflict that doesn't ignite the page; a muddled approach. Perhaps you never acquired a deep understanding of the genre that you were writing in. Perhaps you were unable to gracefully weave your research into your story line.

But usually somewhere deep in your gut you realize that a fatal problem exists. Thus, it's time to—gulp—let go to make way for another project. This doesn't mean that you need to abandon it for all time. Someday when your skills are sharper you might be able to fix the problems. Or a workshop or suggestions from a book doctor will provide solutions that now elude you. But that time is not now, and another story has much more promise, if you will only pull the plug.

Nonfiction Question:

Sometimes it seems as if the truth is elusive. However, truth is the bedrock from which nonfiction writers write. With that said, there are times when writing about a particularly painful topic requires skirting the truth. Perhaps you're writing about abuse or a family secret and you're loath to point a finger at the perpetrator, especially if he or she has reformed. So your approach might be to disguise his or her identity.

There are also practical problems that occur when you write about your past. One difficulty is understandable; few people possess a photographic memory or go through life lugging around a tape recorder. Thus, you don't own a recording of the moment that you were dumped or said something brilliant, unforgivable, or insightful. Often, you're relying on memory, but as any police officer who has ever questioned a witness will tell you, memory is subjective.

So know this: The truth can be stretched but never spun from your imagination. You cannot fabricate scenes or past events that never happened. You cannot ascribe motives to people unless you know these motives to be irrefutable. Search for the truth as best you can, understanding how telling the truth will affect others.

The Writer's Path:

Become someone others can trust. Trustworthiness is important in all aspects of the writing life. If you're working with an editor, do as you say and keep your promises. Make certain that your research is impeccable, your facts irrefutable, and your quotes accurate.

If you are a member of a critique group, make certain that your feedback is balanced, intelligent, and thoughtful. If you feel attacked, find a way to communicate your feelings without launching a counterattack.

When your work is rejected, don't blame anyone. Instead, find the flaws, make the improvements, and move on. Remember, you are not an artist who is forced to sell his or her work in the marketplace; you are a business person who happens to write. So be a business person of impeccable standards, values, and work habits.

18. Bewitched: Mountain/Wind

Do not worry. You have always written before and you will write now.
All you have to do is write one true sentence.
Write the truest sentence that you know.

—Ernest Hemingway

If this hexagram appears, it is likely that your life has taken a downward turn lately, or perhaps a period of disappointment and disillusion has set in. It might even appear as if all has been lost or destroyed. Take heart, because there is hope that you can reverse this trend or transform past mistakes. The answer to reversing things is to understand why the decay happened in the first place, and then accept responsibility to rectify your mistakes. With this understanding and a plan in place, you can turn the page on a new chapter. In this phase there is no room for blame, carelessness, or shortcuts. Instead, patiently make amends and move on.

With effort, you can fulfill your potential. This hexagram also warns you to stay alert, since what appears to be a good thing can be deceptive. Read the fine print.

Fiction Question:

Emotional reversal is a component found in most scenes. A scene begins with the protagonist wanting something, even if it is only a good night's sleep. As the scene unfolds, this goal is achieved or thwarted. During the scene, particularly if there has been a failure to achieve the goal, emotional reversal takes place. Thus, the character's emotional state at the beginning of the scene is quite different from his emotions at the conclusion.

For example, a scene with potential lovers getting together could begin with one or both feeling excited, anticipating a pleasant evening. But then things go wrong. He confesses that he's not officially divorced, or, after the second cocktail, she confesses that she cannot get over her ex. The evening that began with bright promise turns sour. Emotional reversal provides the sort of roller coaster ride that readers crave.

Nonfiction Question:

Writing nonfiction for an audience is not a license to vent. That's what therapy and confiding in a close friend are for. When a writer has been hurt, wronged, or ripped off, he is often tempted to explore the pain on the page, to be heard when perhaps he has been silenced. But this hexagram suggests another approach that is both simple and difficult. The way lies in forgiveness.

Forgiveness is not a religious concept; it is something far easier. Forgiveness happens when the person who has wronged you no longer has the power to cause pain. You have moved on; you are busy with life and writing, and the hurt no longer holds you captive. Let go and keep moving forward, and rewards will come. You might want to write about this process, rather than the pain that once held you captive.

The Writer's Path:

You are at a crucial point in your writing life. You must proceed with care and rectify past mistakes so that you are no longer blocked. Ruthlessly and honestly assess your weaknesses and self-sabotage. It might be helpful to find another person to point out the flaws in your writing, thinking, or habits if you're unable to see them objectively.

Yet knowing your limitations and correcting them are two different things. The first is painful, the second daunting. The trick here is to accept responsibility, act like an adult, and use all your adult skills to repair what has gone wrong. Use the same determination with which you've tackled other life challenges and apply it to your writing. No matter your level of skill, you can improve—and you must. Renovate, renew yourself, and plan a new beginning.

---

19. Onward: Earth/Lake

Good work doesn't happen with inspiration. It comes with constant, often tedious and deliberate effort. If your vision of a writer involves sitting in a cafe, sipping an aperitif with one's fellow geniuses, become a drunk. It's easier and far less exhausting.

—William Hefferman

It's a new day! The energy of the earth is supportive and nurturing while the waters of the lake are soft and quiet. This can be the best of times, but danger still might lurk. Traditional interpretations for Hexagram 19 warn of problems in the eighth month and anything related to water—a flood, slipping on a wet floor, a swimming or boating accident.

Yet something energizing and electric is in the air, as intoxicating as spring-time. With this sense of new beginnings and positive forces, make certain that you don't squander its energy. Don't try to hurry success or force your will. Just as spring blossoms must first winter over, proceed one step at a time and don't skip any steps along the way. Keep moving toward your goals; make necessary changes; avoid complacency. Also be alert for small slippages and make immediate corrections before things deteriorate.

This hexagram also has a special significance for dealing with relationships. Pay attention to how your actions affect others, and see the big picture. If it's possible to delegate tasks, do so now. Finally, Onward warns that people with evil purposes will fail or be exposed, so approach everyone and everything with good intentions.

Fiction Question:

In real life, random and tragic events occur: an auto accident; a frightening diagnosis; the loss of someone close. In fiction, however, nothing is random because every aspect of the story is interlinked by causality. This causal connection is especially linked to the protagonist's actions. Think of dominoes; one topples over and the others fall too.

A terrific example of causality that is intimately linked to character is illustrated in Colin Harrison's literary thriller, *The Havana Room*. The inciting incident is the accidental death of a child at the protagonist's home. This tragedy creates a cascade of repercussions, and in short order the protagonist loses his standing in the community, his job, his wife and son, his home, and his reason for living. Drifting, he finds a community in a busy restaurant and then, by meeting the employees and patrons, he is pulled into danger and a mystery until he is forced to reclaim the man he was before the child died.

But he would never have been lured into the mysterious Havana Room without a string of events that pushed him there. Look for other models of causality in the novels you read and keep asking yourself how events in your stories can cause more events and troubles for your protagonist.

Nonfiction Question:

Many memoirists struggle with how much truth they should reveal when they write their life stories. Most writers fear exposing secrets, especially those involving family members or family skeletons. And memoirists worry about the repercussions of these stories once the revelations are published.

But there is a simple litmus test that you can apply: question your purpose for writing. If you're writing to settle a score or to tell your side of a story, then this hexagram warns that your project might backfire on you. If you see yourself as a victim in a situation and feel compelled to write about it, you'll find sympathy within your immediate circle, but readers will see through your motives. The only way to write about pain is when you are not so emotionally involved, or perhaps have taken responsibility for your role in the situation.

For some writers, excavating the past and exposing themselves as vulnerable and tainted can work. David Sedaris makes a living from books and essays that shine a spotlight into the shadows of his life and on everyone he meets. But if you read closely, you'll notice that Sedaris has mastered his art. While his words are at times scathing and satiric, he's also compassionate and self-deprecating, and wraps his jabs in humor and tenderness.

The Writer's Path:

Good news is in the air. If you've been waiting to approach an editor or agent, now is the time. If you've been putting off trying to sell a new idea or marketing yourself, your timing is perfect—go for it. If any opportunity for promotion appears, pursue it ruthlessly. Also, if a partnership or collaboration suggests itself now, give it careful consideration because it has potential. The single warning in this hexagram is not to rush shoddy work into the market-place and not to expect instant results. Keep your eye on long-term success, not get-rich-quick schemes.

The deeper meaning in this hexagram relates to understanding that you are a writer and the world needs your stories, heart, and talent. Take your place and be counted.

20. Contemplation: Wind/Earth

I write for the same reason I breathe—because if I didn't, I would die.

—Isaac Asimov

The wind sweeping over the earth connects us to a quiet force that lies within each of us. This hexagram suggests looking down from above or watching. Thus, if possible, view your life from a fresh perspective and notice how others react to you.

Focus and calm are required if you are to work your way through this situation. As you benefit from a new view, search for aspects you might have overlooked. It is crucial that you think ahead and make decisions based on a broad overview. If possible, detach yourself and remain unemotional about whatever needs to be done. Listen, and others will listen to you. Whatever you know or learn, use this knowledge to help others. Also—and this is important—translate your knowledge into action.

Fiction Question:

While fiction is based on conflict that is dramatized by action, a story cannot press forward at full speed all the time. As in real life, the story world needs moments of quiet and normalcy. Perhaps the protagonist eats a meal, chats with a friend, or drives to the location of the next scene. These quieter moments give the reader a chance to catch his breath and control the pacing.

There will be few quiet moments or pauses in the final scenes, so these are interspersed mostly in the middle after the story question is established and the story world is adequately drawn. A writer can also take advantage of these lulls to slip in exposition or flashbacks, and can reflect on themes or events that have already happened. So from time to time, pause for a breather so that the reader can set down the book.

Nonfiction Question:

Writers throughout time have tracked their memories for inspiration. The ancient Greeks so believed in the power of memory that they named a goddess, Mnemosyne, after it. She was the daughter of Earth and Sky and mother of the Muses, and was called on for inspiration. Some artists believe that memory is where all art begins. For writers, remembrance of childhood can unleash their natural voice and excavate truth, meaning, and imagination.

The memoirist needs a way to track down those treasures hiding in the dark recesses of memory. You cannot merely wander from forgetfulness to remembrance, or stumble onto the past; you need tools to mine it.

In this cave of memory, uncover your friends, beloved pets, your third grade teacher, and the outfits that you wore in her classroom. Artifacts are stored here—dolls, games, and bicycles—and these items whisper from your childhood. Yet memory doesn't equal nostalgia or sentimentality. While tracking your memory, you're hunting the stuff of daily life, the grit and pain, tucked in along with laughter, loss, and regret. So approach the past with a questioning mind. Dust off the memory, and then examine all sides of it, using the lamplight of adult knowledge. Remove the filters, and notice the emotions that arise.

The Writer's Path:

The message here is simple: don't take it personally. Often, when a writer crafts stories from his own life, he feels judged based on the life he has led. Or if he's spent years writing a novel, he feels as if the characters are his children. When someone rejects his novel, he feels like his family has been murdered. In reality, he is being judged on the craft that he has applied to the subject at hand.

The publishing business is a tough one and only those who can work through rejection and failure will survive. In the ordinary world you will likely receive more accolades and rewards for your hard work. In the ordinary world you will not work for long periods without payment. Writing by its nature requires an unpaid apprenticeship. And then you're often disappointed once you start sending your work out. It can be heartbreaking.

But don't crumble now. If the feedback you've received tells you that your work is shoddy or unsophisticated, correct those problems. Find a way to improve no matter what it takes, and don't take it personally.

---

21. Biting Through: Fire/Thunder

I get a fine warm feeling when I'm doing well, but that pleasure
is pretty much negated by the pain of getting started each day.
Let's face it, writing is hell.

—William Styron

Biting Through recommends determination and immediate, decisive action. In ancient texts this hexagram depicted a jaw and suggested that a person must bite through a problem. This problem has been brewing for some time and you cannot ignore it any longer. No matter the issue, it requires swift movement because you've thought about it long enough.

If you consider how fire and thunder might come together to create lightning, you'll be on track with the meaning of this hexagram. Biting Through can also refer to legal problems, power struggles, or injustice. There are times to ponder or move cautiously. This is not one of them. Nor should you give in to wishful thinking or childish longings. Take the plunge, stop procrastinating, and move ahead with confidence.

Fiction Question:

Jack Bickham's book, *The 38 Most Common Fiction Writing Mistakes (And How To Avoid Them)* includes a chapter called "Don't Write About Wimps." Bickham writes:

> Fiction writers too often forget that interesting characters are almost always characters who are active—risk-takers—highly motivated toward a goal. Many a story has been wrecked at the outset because the writer chose to write about the wrong kind of person—a character of the type we sometimes call a wimp.

Fiction is about proactive types and when it comes to protagonists, there are wimps and then there are nonwimps. And you must write about the latter. Nonwimps simply make things happen in a story. When a nonwimp is central to a story, the action never stops. Nonwimps don't retreat or shed tears when story events pile on the misery. They might choke back tears, but they don't sigh pitifully, fret endlessly, or consult their therapist when the chips are down. True, they sometimes panic, doubt, and worry, but they take it in stride and plunge ahead. Nonwimps are relentless seekers of truth and justice; they never give up, and create outcomes that make fiction better than reality.

Nonfiction Question:

When it comes to writing from our own lives, the lesson is simple: go where the pain is. And the pain is often based on loss. In loss we face our mortality and loneliness, and in coping with and triumphing over these losses, we are unmasked. While traveling these bitter roads, we disclose what it is to be fragile, but also how to find solace and strength in the midst of life's difficulties.

A terrific example of coping with loss is found in Scott Russell Sanders' essay "The Inheritance of Tools." His first sentence sets the tone for the pain and insights that follow: "At just about the hour when my father died, soon after dawn one February morning when ice coated the windows like cataracts, I banged my thumb with a hammer."

He uses extended metaphors and analogies to underline his themes about what a father teaches and means to his son. The hammer he banged his thumb with belonged to his father and grandfather and it had built houses, barns, chicken coops, jewelry boxes, and doll furniture. He describes it, telling the reader, "It gives off the sort of dull sheen you see on fast creek water in the shade."

The essay traces the lessons passed on from father to son: how to hammer in a nail, how to use a handsaw, how to cut wood straight, how to miter a joint, and how to be a patient and admiring teacher. Sanders describes how he went on to master more tools. Then he returns to the moment he learns of his father's death:

> For several hours I paced around inside my house, upstairs and
> down, in and out of every room, looking for the right door to
> open and knowing there was no such door. My wife and children

followed me and wrapped me in arms and backed away again, circling and staring as if I were on fire. Where was the door, the door, the door? I kept wondering.

Then he returns to his building project and what was bequeathed, an inheritance of tools.

The Writer's Path:

If you have chosen this hexagram, it is likely that an inner storm has been brewing and it is based on a particular relationship. R.L. Wing, an authority on the *I Ching*, says, " Personal relationships without defined guidelines, reasonable expectations, reciprocal considerations and clear plans for the future are now in danger of dissolving in the chaos being generated by the current situation."

The answer to this situation is to set personal boundaries as a way to protect and care for yourself. It forces you to take responsibility for how people treat you. Learning how to set boundaries teaches you how to communicate with directness and honesty and to be self-protective. Erect them so that you can tell others when they are acting in ways that are unacceptable.

Setting boundaries with strangers is, of course, easy, but the more intimate your relationship, the more difficult it is to ask for what you need. While setting boundaries, you must also apply them to yourself. Biting Through requires that you unmask your own delusions, poor judgments, or rationalizations. Wing warns, "Equivocal or vague principles, as a rule, will make of your life an undirected, uninspired, meaningless act." Use tough love on yourself and your bad habits. Adhere to standards that you can be proud of.

22. Grace: Mountain/Fire

Writing is a struggle against silence.

—Carlos Fuentes

A fire is burning at the base of the mountain and the flames are illuminating the mountain with a rare beauty. If you're careful, the fire won't cause damage. Grace teaches you patience to proceed without impetuousness because positive aspects are at work. You are also reminded to follow proper etiquette and pay attention to your social behavior.

You'll find yourself inspired and in flow with ideas and satisfying outcomes. However, if you're impatient and rush ahead before the necessary steps are set in place, the results might be disastrous.

Grace also reminds you that you'll achieve the best results by making small changes or nibbling away at a problem. It's not the time for sweeping reforms or grandiose schemes. If you're in the midst of some difficulty, using tact and charm will accomplish more than confrontations. Strive for inner grace and beauty, not outer trappings. Develop qualities that will serve you as a writer and a person of integrity—in other words, true grace.

Fiction Question:

Refinement and carefully honed writing are called for. It's not a time for drastic rewrites and changes. Fiction writers are often more concerned with plot than they are with words. But never forget that editors are word people. They love words. They understand the power of language, and notice your care in stringing words together. Editors sigh at the beauty of a well-chosen metaphor, a poignant image, or a powerful analogy.

Your level of skill with words will be telegraphed within the first sentences of your manuscript. And if you have not crafted beautiful sentences, you cannot tell a story. So start with the humblest of your tools—words—and scrutinize your sentences to make sure that each word is precise and perfect.

Nonfiction Question:

Add music to your words. Literary nonfiction is set apart from mere reporting by the beauty of language, the depth of themes, and the meaning that infuses every word and image. Music means that the writing employs pleasing sounds that appeal to the inner ear. When a person reads, he hears the sounds of words and sentence constructions inside his head. With this in mind, write to create pleasing sounds. Music is delivered by many means: alliteration, repetition, varying sentence lengths and constructions, fragments, run-on sentences, metaphor, and other charms.

Imparting music comes naturally to some writers, while others must consciously inject sound appeal. Begin by mastering one technique at a time, such as simile. After you write a chapter or essay, edit it, and then print it out. While reading it, notice where the writing is flat, where the ideas don't quite take hold. When you find these trouble spots, ask yourself, "How can I deepen the meaning here? Can I make a comparison here?" Adding music is also the art of making apt comparisons. In these comparisons we add another layer of meaning, enhancing the melody line.

The Writer's Path:

Grace suggests that you act on inspirations, pursuing small projects and focusing on sentences or paragraphs. It also suggests that you find contentment in your daily writing routine and small successes. Spend time improving your style and voice and then notice how they enhance the whole. It's also a time for collecting your ideas for future projects into one place—perhaps a file or notebook.

Grace suggests that it is not time for your social life or environment to interfere with your writing goals. If you have a book or project to promote, it's a great time to do so. But don't allow the outer world to steal too much time away from your desk. It's a ripe time for success in your writing, so don't fritter this energy away on nonessentials.

23. Discarding: Mountain/Earth

In composing, as a general rule, run a pen through every other word you have written; you have no idea what vigor it will give your style.

—Sydney Smith

The mountain is stable and enduring, rooted to the earth yet creating a situation in which there is insecurity and a power struggle. This hexagram is also called Falling Away, Splitting Apart, or Peeling Off. Think about these meanings. You are likely in the midst of a deteriorating situation; you may feel that you are overwhelmed or that things are spinning out of control. Caution is called for. Avoid blowups, entanglements, and confrontations because the consequences could be unsettling. It's important not to struggle against the inevitable. Instead, lay low and wait patiently for signs that it is time to move on.

Another important lesson is that some elements in your life no longer serve you, and it is time to get rid of them. Face the fact that a cycle is ending and let go when necessary to make way for the new. You might need to discard bad habits, relationships that you've outgrown, or projects that are floundering. Discernment is called for; you must make choices about what goes, what stays, or if it's best to simply bide your time and let things blow over.

No matter your decision, you need to make it with extreme caution. To act rashly now will backfire. Your problems are not going to disappear on their own; you're required to root them out and face the truth. It's also a time for conserving your strength and resources for the next big push.

Fiction Question:

A first draft doesn't necessarily need to be good; it merely needs to get written so that you can tackle the difficult job of writing the second draft. When editing your initial draft, read your manuscript and question what is missing, what is hackneyed, and make certain you've tied up all the plot threads. While evaluating the second draft, make the broad strokes before you deepen the story, then in the third draft, copy edit and perfect the language.

Before approaching your second draft, let it cool a bit. Experts like Stephen King suggest leaving it in a file drawer for several months. While that practice might work for a dynamo like King, most of us don't have the luxury of quite so much cooling time. But taking at least a week or a month away from the story guarantees that when you approach it again you'll see it with fresh eyes. Your next step is to print it and read it in a place other than where you wrote it. You want your experience of reading it to be different from your experience of writing it.

With a pen handy, first read it for completeness. Ask yourself these questions: Have you launched the story at the last possible moment before slipping in the backstory? Is your protagonist's backstory gracefully woven in and does it affect the outcome of the front story? Are there setting and visual elements in every scene? Do you build and add conflict as the story progresses?

Then examine the structure. Do surprises and complications keep sending the story off in new directions, while it remains true to its chief conflict? Have you written mostly in scenes? Does your protagonist have a goal in each scene? Do you use cliffhangers and unfinished business to end some scenes so that they thrust forward?

Ask yourself hard questions about the ending. Have you tied up the sub-plots? Does the ending deliver emotion and answer the promise of the story? Does the story provide a surprise that's too contrived? Have you provided a denouement or ended at a moment of high drama? Is the epilogue necessary, or are you simply unable to finish the story without it?

Nonfiction Question:

Mitchell Ivers, former managing editor of Random House, wrote, "Style should not be thought of as an end to itself. It is a result of a series of choices of voice, tone, diction, structure, grammar and usage—that depend on purpose and appropriateness. Putting style in almost always clutters writing up; removing clutter gives writing style."

Clutter comes in so many guises that sometimes it's difficult to spot it in your own work. Clutter occurs in intensifiers and qualifiers. Omit words such as: really, absolutely, terribly, very, quite, rather, sort of, kind of, a little, generally, hopefully, overall, rather, particularly, reportedly, so-called, deeply, truly, sincerely, unfortunately, especially, totally, somewhat, exactly.

Beware of prepositions piling up. Little words and prepositional phrases often clog sentences and smother your nouns and verbs. In general, sentences consist of a noun, verb, and object. Nouns and verbs are the most important parts of the sentences, especially verbs, which are the motors that push the sentences forward.

Prepositions allow distance between important words in a sentence and appear before a noun. They often convey spatial relationships, telling us where X is in relationship to Y. They appear singularly or in clusters and sometimes act as conjunctions or adverbs: about, above, across, after, against, ahead, of, along, among, apart from, around, as, as for, as well as, aside from, at, away from, before, behind, below, beside, besides, between, beyond, but, by, by means of, down, during, except, for, from, in, in back of, in front of, inside, instead of, into, like, near, of, off, on, onto, out, out of, outside, over, past, since, through, throughout, till, to, together with, toward, under, until, up, up to, upon, with, within, without, with regard to. If your sentences contain strings of prepositional phrases, strip most sentences down to their most important components whenever possible.

Analyze your style word by word, sentence by sentence. Ask yourself if every word is the best one available for meaning, rhythm, sound, and connotation.

The Writer's Path:

The principles of feng shui provide practical solutions for writers. Feng shui is a Chinese practice of arranging objects in an environment to achieve balance and an optimal flow of energy. Feng shui masters claim that living by its basic rules will enhance all aspects of life, while ignoring them will cause sorrow and misfortune. Meaning "wind-water," it is based on *chi*—dragon's breath—the life-bringing energy of the universe. Every object, living or inanimate, has an energy field and can influence chi.

It's important to be inspired and calmed by your workspace and habits. If you are surrounded by reminders of failure and doubt, you'll be dragged down. If you live amid noise, chaos, or just plain ugliness, your energy will be drained. On the other hand, if you live among beauty, order, and objects that speak to the sweetness of life, you'll flourish.

One of the most important principles of feng shui is to clear the clutter from your life. Dirt, clutter, and disorder create stagnant chi and block the flow of positive energy. If your office and living space are chaotic or crowded with too much furniture or belongings, or your paperwork is a mess, become ruthless about clearing out everything that is no longer useful, and then restore order. Remember that as you toss and file, you are symbolically removing unwanted barriers in your life and creating harmony out of chaos.

---

24. The Turning Point: Earth/Thunder

Success comes to a writer as a rule,
so gradually that it is always something of a shock to him to look back
and realize the heights to which he has climbed.

—P. G. Wodehouse

Finally, after a time of setbacks and perhaps losses, a new cycle is here. Below is the bellicose activity of thunder while above, the earth provides solidity and nourishment. This hexagram is associated with the Winter Solstice, when the dark days of winter are giving way and new light is returning. The result is renewed energy and optimism. It signifies rebirth, renewal, and returning.

Although your optimism might be long overdue, don't blunder ahead blindly. Instead, understand the reasons for the problems that you've recently survived and use that wisdom to guide your next careful steps. It's a good time for reflection and making plans and decisions. If situations or projects have deteriorated, there is still time to make corrections. The Turning Point is also a time to use fresh approaches to ongoing situations and relationships.

Fiction Question:

In most fiction, by the end of the story your character's fortunes will have changed. How he thinks and acts will change. How he perceives the world will change. The middle of the story is a prolonged setup for this necessary transformation to take place. And the best way to make this transformation believable is to demonstrate that your character overcomes obstacles and gains confidence even as he is exhausted by the challenges of the story events.

The middle of a novel usually provides the strongest turning point in the story. This event sends the plot skittering off into a new direction and revives the action. This turning point will surprise and intrigue the reader, but at the same time seem like a natural consequence of forces that were set in motion in the opening. At least one dramatic reversal, complication, or, unpleasant setback usually occurs in the middle.

Another way to think of the middle is that it is a point of no return that triggers the events that will lead to the climax. The structure of the F. Scott Fitzgerald's *The Great Gatsby* can illustrate this point. The novel has only nine chapters and each is densely packed with tension and details that further the story. Chapter five opens with Nick returning home at night and noticing that Gatsby's house is lit up as if on fire. Nick goes over to talk with Gatsby and they hatch a plan to invite Daisy to Nick's house for tea. Nick then phones her, extends the invitation, and asks her not to bring her husband, Tom.

In the scene that takes place when Gatsby and Daisy meet, the reader witnesses Gatsby's vulnerability and how his desire for her is at the heart of the story. Once they are together again, their renewed relationship leads to a tragic and perhaps inevitable conclusion. The lesson here is that in the middle, new problems or situations arise, providing further momentum and renewing the story as it heads towards a dramatic conclusion.

Nonfiction Question:

In every life there are crossroads where we are forced to make difficult choices. To marry or not. To divorce or not. To have children or not. To accept the job or turn down the promotion. To give in to temptation or resist it. To move to a distant city or stay in your hometown.

These crossroads, while sometimes difficult, are fertile grounds for exploring on the page. Readers will be reminded of their own struggles as you wrestle with yours. Create a list of the most difficult decisions of your life or your biggest regrets. In this list you'll likely find heartbreak and wisdom as well as joys and strength.

Reflect too on the times and ways that you reinvented yourself, the times you believed in yourself and it paid off, and the times you bounced back after adversity. Remember these turnaround times so that you can illustrate what it means to be human, what it means to grow.

The Writer's Path:

There is a source available that you can call on when your hopes dwindle or energy fades. Some writers have spiritual or religious beliefs that they use to bolster themselves when times are hard. Others find a source in nature, in their intuition, or in the words of fellow writers. No matter where you find your strength and inspiration, it is vital that you tap it when times are hard.

This hexagram recommends that you turn to the source and settle into the work at hand. It is not a time for mingling with friends or playing at life. Focus on the project that has the greatest potential. Work in trust, yet ask for guidance. The Turning Point also suggests that there is a great benefit now in being reflective, in conserving your energy, and especially in understanding how your mistakes were created.

———

25. Appropriateness: Heaven/Thunder

To imagine yourself inside another person ... is what a story writer does in every piece of work; it is his first step, and his last too, I suppose.

—Eudora Welty

Hexagram 25 is one of the more difficult to translate directly. It means "not untruthful" and some *I Ching* experts translate it as Integrity, the Unexpected, or Without Falsehood. According to Chinese philosophy there are times for plunging in and joining and there are times to dodge entanglements. This period calls for stepping back, avoiding complications, and correcting your course.

If possible, stay out of people's way and detach yourself from situations and relationships. If a problem arises, act according to your scruples and values. If you choose shortcuts or are talked into a shady deal, the consequences will be unfortunate. Instead, be guided by fairness and appropriateness. While many things can change in the course of a lifetime, truth remains the same.

Sometimes you have too many choices before you, too many ideas you long to pursue. Select goals with care, guided by your intuition. Know your motivations and ask yourself if they are honorable. If they are, then follow through with intense effort. This work must stem from your essential nature, and must not be undertaken simply to please others.

Fiction Question:

Fiction is about interesting people in situations of jeopardy. This danger exists in fiction in varying degrees, from life-or-death stakes to a character on a path of inner transformation revealed in a quieter framework. Whatever your plot, fictional characters must act with logic and consistency. In the real world, people are unpredictable and can exhibit wild mood swings and irrational behaviors. In the fictional world, people act according to the laws of the fictional universe and in keeping with their core traits.

One way to achieve a character's logical behavior is to craft him or her with a set of primary traits. The most prominent of them (about three to five) will make up the protagonist's core personality. These traits are based on the needs of the plot and can be such attributes as: resourcefulness, toughness, cautiousness, wiliness, brilliance, persistence, inquisitiveness, compassion, recklessness, sophistication, naïveté, charisma, reticence, smoothness, and cunning.

When your protagonist first appears on the page, these traits are immediately identifiable and provide a personality foundation that the reader can track and that the story hinges on. For example, a brave character will be forced to prove his bravery or a brilliant detective will use his brainpower to solve a difficult case. And while many stories are about transformation, these foundational aspects of character will not change. Your brave hero is not going to flee when the bullets start flying. Your wily detective isn't going to throw in the towel because the case is too complicated. Dominant traits provide the backbone for both main and secondary characters and direct how they'll act and react to story events.

Nonfiction Question:

Nonfiction requires that the writer make choices about the most appropriate framework for his message. Some sentiments are conveyed best in a poem; some information belongs in a journalism article. For exploring the human condition, an essay often works best. Passions and convictions can be appropriate for an opinion piece or letter to the editor, but if woven around anecdotes, can also work as an essay. Some ideas are best suited to an article as opposed to a book because they simply don't have the depth that it takes to stretch to two hundred pages.

Over time, you'll make these choices based on experience and the reactions of readers. But here is a clue: the scope of your information will determine the format you choose. A simple idea such as a single memory of childhood doesn't need a whole book to cover it. But if you had an interesting childhood amid eccentrics and maniacs, then a memoir is suited to your memories.

The Writer's Path:

Often, when a writer sits down to craft a complex project such as a novel, the difficulty is daunting. Some writers give up before they begin, while others bog down after the first inspiration and excitement wanes. In Anne Lamott's *Bird by Bird* she advises setting a one-by-one inch picture frame near your computer as a reminder that you need to write only enough words to fill that tiny space. Using such a narrow and finite focus, it's easy to relax and craft a few words. Then a few more.

This is not to say that grand goals and plans are not laudable or even necessary to the writing life. But if you've never written fiction before, perhaps start by taking a class, or writing a short story or a character sketch. If you dream of a byline in *The New Yorker*, that's terrific. More power to you. But if you've never been published before, you need to start with your community newspaper or a web site. You need to build your craft word by word and fill in the small spaces.

---

26. Focus: Mountain/Heaven

In America, the race goes to the loud, the solemn, the hustler.
If you think you're a great writer, you must say that you are.

—Gore Vidal

The weight of the mountain looms over the heavens, so imagine mountain peaks among the clouds. The ancient Chinese believed that the clouds were accumulating rain and that this accumulation was auspicious. Thus, be ready for advancement and anticipate good news because the timing is ripe. There is excitement in the air and you might feel adventuresome, independent, and ready for your next step.

This is a time to analyze and select a project that has the greatest potential. With focus, you can expect positive outcomes. Ask for help, but if none is forthcoming, you will find the resources within to handle challenges and complete projects. If you need information or data, gather it now. Use every moment of every day to push ahead and let others know that you're on track with your plans.

This hexagram generally signals good news and indicates that it is possible to make a living as a writer. But the *I Ching* warns about a headlong rush into things. Consider your next steps from a place of inner quiet. Once you've accumulated the necessary information, reach out, promote yourself, and explore your potential.

If you've paid your dues, you can plunge ahead, meet new writers, take risks, and enjoy endless possibilities. As you work productively, keep on top of the small details, pace yourself, and stay organized so that you don't lose momentum.

Fiction Question:

The first draft is usually the most fun to write. It's as if the wind is at your back and ideas are bubbling up, characters are taking shape, and you feel an invigorating momentum. Once you're pushing ahead with energy and inspiration, write fast and write often, staying focused. When you're not at your desk, carry a notebook that is devoted exclusively to your story, and every time an idea occurs, jot it down.

If you run into an obstacle while working on the first draft, write past it. Jot notes about the scene where you're stuck and move on to the next. Don't get bogged down with endless questioning or rewrites; your job here is to lay the foundation and explore the main characters. If you get seriously bogged down it's time to get to know your characters better.

Start by creating a dossier or biography of your protagonist and antagonist. With this knowledge, their secret desires and deepest fears emerge. Knowing your protagonist's greatest fear is a powerful tool for shaping a story. If the main characters still do not come to life, experiment. Try writing in each character's journal or diary. Your characters might exchange letters or emails. Interview your character, questioning him about childhood events that most shaped him. Now, it's unlikely that these letters or all the details in the biography will show up in your pages. Instead, you are creating the intimacy of the character's voice, background, and motivation from which the story will emerge.

Nonfiction Question:

The best nonfiction brims with life from the larger world. While nonfiction is often introspective, it must also include the objects, events, and surroundings that can be experienced through the senses. This is the stuff of life, and without it nonfiction is shallow. So tap into your stores of memory and creativity, but also the world at large. Make your writing tangible and solid, especially if you're writing about abstract concepts.

The best writers are collectors, noting the passing of seasons and light and sky in all their shadings. They live their days on a constant surveillance mission, questioning, eavesdropping, and noticing. They spot the details that make nonfiction breathe, but also find the significance of small moments amid a busy world. They collect things, examples, and artifacts and learn the names of everything in their world. Then this stuff of life is deftly threaded into a story. Finally, they're also able to step back and gain a larger view, reflecting on how politics, eras, and trends shape the world.

Show readers not only your heart, but the complicated place in which we all live together, stamped with your particular brand of clarity. Readers slow down for specific information and get bogged down in abstractions. Help them find themselves amid your stories, amid a life that brims with passion and meaning.

The Writer's Path:

Many writers become distracted by the mystique of the writing life. They wrongly assume that it means isolation, misery, and loneliness. Others fantasize a romantic, garret-dwelling, latté-sipping lifestyle in Parisian cafes while the publishing world begs permission to print their jewels of wisdom. Both viewpoints are flawed.

Most of us are called to writing because it chooses us. But writing is a business, one that demands discipline, networking with people in the industry, and delivering professional-quality products. As you write, develop the same habits as a successful lawyer, doctor, or plumber. You deliver on time, you stay on top of the latest developments in your trade, and you put in long hours.

It can be notoriously difficult to break into publishing, especially if you don't have any contacts, what R.L. Wing terms "useful connections." Writers need to meet sources, editors, agents, and experts in all fields to keep the income flowing. Writers' conferences, book signings, classes, book expos are all places where writers gather and exchange ideas. Be adventurous in how you reach out—create a blog, write a newsletter, exchange emails with other writers. Grow your circle and the rewards will follow. You never know when a pro is going to give you a go-ahead at a conference or through a chance encounter.

—

27. Nourishment: Mountain/Thunder

Writing is the only thing that, when I do it,
I don't feel I should be doing something else.

—Gloria Steinem

The ancient sages believed that Hexagram 27 was related to all aspects of nourishment and that it referred to the proper feeding of oneself and others. Feed yourself from the many aspects of life, including the arts and nature. If you don't normally take care of your body, this is the time to correct those mistakes. If you're called on to care for another person, weigh this commitment and whether this person will pass along your generosity. Weigh also if you're an inspiring presence, a genuinely encouraging and supportive friend. If you are a person who gives generously, your generosity will come back to you.

Nourishment also refers to how you think, and advises that you correct destructive thought patterns. If you're a "glass is half empty" type, now is the time to right this cynicism. If you're prone to anxiety, seek calm. Learn to relax in the midst of pressure and to express passions without burning out. It's also advisable to avoid indulgences and extravagance.

Fiction Question:

You read fiction for pleasure and the delicious intimacy of slipping into a character's life; if you write fiction you must learn to analyze it. In examining an author's techniques, you learn how to implement your own. For example, it's extremely helpful to notice how quickly a writer jumps in and out of scenes. Pay attention to dialogue, and the underlying tension or conflict embedded in it. Examine the subtler elements of fiction, such as transitions, theme, and premise. Notice when the author has included flashbacks, how they illuminate the story, and their overall proportion in the story.

Notice too when and how subplots are added, and how they affect character development and the outcome of the plot. Scrutinize scene and chapter endings, noting how they create thrusters—cliffhangers and other devices that push the story ahead. Since pacing is often a problem for beginning writers, pay attention to when the story slows down and when it speeds up. Chart how the writer varies the pace and when he inserts sequels to scenes. Finally, study the ending and how the story events culminate; note how many pages are designated to the ending, how characters are changed by the story events, and how the subplots are wrapped up.

Nonfiction Question:

Inspiration is found in our lives and the world around us, but if you don't examine the work of published writers, you are missing important lessons. The best memoirs teach how narrative techniques are used to reveal a life and how to find themes or meaning within the events of a life. A well-written memoir can teach how to move back and forth in time and how to describe eras.

Essays should be studied for how they are structured, how the theme is delivered, how the opening hooks the reader's interest, and how narrative techniques are used. Notice the writer's style devices, how metaphors are used to enhance meaning, and how themes are explored through specific data.

The Writer's Path:

In *The Artist's Way,* Julia Cameron recommends the practice of "artist dates," whereby artists step out into the world alone to recharge their creative juices, or, as she suggests, to "stock the pond." She writes:

> An artist date is a block of time, perhaps two hours weekly, especially set aside and committed to nurturing your creative consciousness, your inner artist. In its most primary form, the artist date is an excursion, a play date that you preplan and defend against all interlopers.

An artist date can take many forms—seeing a play or movie, strolling through a junk store, visiting a gallery or museum, walking along the beach, or hiking in a forest. The idea is that you feed your imagination with sights and sounds or quiet. Since writers are constantly pouring out words, filling your imagination with new images will recharge your creative batteries.

——

28. Overload: Lake/Wind

An absolutely necessary part of a writer's equipment, almost as necessary as talent, is the ability to stand up under punishment, both the punishment the world hands out and the punishment he inflicts upon himself.

—Irwin Shaw

This hexagram features the soft yin lake over the sweeping force of the wind below. This reversed position, sometimes called Critical Mass, indicates great activity. It might portray a situation out of balance, about to tumble out of control, or it can refer to something exceeding its capacity. It also suggests that the situation is unusual and your reactions to it must be measured.

Perhaps a crisis is unfolding and you feel burdened and smothered by responsibility. A solution is called for because your predicament is indefensible. Determine if you are the cause of the problem or if it stems from a relationship. Examine all factors involved and correct your attitudes and approach to life. Act quickly, but avoid aggression or excess force.

This might also be a period of transition or when a structure is falling apart. Creating a plan to handle things will be extremely helpful, as will acting based on your priorities. The situation suggests that flexibility is the key to dealing with things. It also suggests that if you can survive trauma or crisis, you can handle anything. Don't be afraid to act alone if it's called for. Ask yourself if the situation honors you and your goals and plans. If not, move on. You are a survivor. Don't be afraid to leave what you have outgrown.

Fiction Question:

The climax in fiction must provide the strongest emotion, potency, and reader satisfaction. It is the inevitable and rational result of all that has gone before. The climax also releases the reader from the buildup of tension and provides insights into what all the conflict has been about. It is also a point of no return, and after this moment the protagonist's life will never be the same again.

But while the climax must provide high drama, it should not be melodramatic, prolonged, or sensational. A climax is often a showdown of some kind: within the self or with another character, society, or nature. Most of the extra characters have been whisked offstage, leaving the main characters to provide the climax. In these crucial moments the writing is pared down to the essentials, and if possible, most of the subplots and loose ends have been tidied up beforehand.

The action in the climax depends on the genre. An action story requires that the final confrontation contain physical danger. In mainstream fiction the protagonist's unbearable misery or difficult choices often demand a decision, self-discovery, or recognition of something important. No matter if your climax is a blazing shootout or a dramatic moment of realization, make certain that it stems from your protagonist's deepest core.

Nonfiction Question:

Like fiction, nonfiction essays require a structure to provide the foundation that keeps the work from running amok. Many writers know what they want to say, but creating the structure to plug their thoughts into is another matter.

A helpful structure for essays looks like this:

1. Your opening paragraphs create a hook. This can be an intriguing quote or dialogue, action, an anecdote, sensory details, or a strong image. A hook plants a question in the reader's mind—often what's

going to happen next—that demands that he keep reading. The opening also introduces the subject, establishes the voice and tone, and hints at conflict, tension, or a question that will be answered.

2. Your next paragraphs provide context for the subject. The reader needs to know where he is and why.

3. Return to the anecdote, scene, or information in the opening and add a new scene or anecdote. This section provides more narrative and immediacy.

4. Add information to flesh out the essay. Weave in statistics, backstory, experts' opinions, and facts. But remember, a little goes a long way and an essay is not a report.

5. End by returning to the lead or slip in another intriguing device. Conclude with a powerful quote, a lingering image, or sensory details. The best endings in nonfiction persist in the reader's mind and have a palpable quality.

The Writer's Path:

Your writing path is being hindered by too many responsibilities. Accept this fact and make adjustments. Examine your schedule and note what obligations claim your time and focus. In the light of this understanding, set new priorities. Shift your attitude and examine what hinders your writing goals and what contributes to your success.

Another issue of Overload is that somebody is making excess demands or is exaggerating his feelings or needs. Although it is difficult, you must confront him and negotiate a healthier relationship. It's not necessary to be excessive, but firmness is required. Stand up for your needs and dreams even if you are forced to go it alone. If you have the strength to make the changes called for, your success is guaranteed.

29. Extreme Danger: Water/Water

All suffering is bearable if it is seen as part of a story.

—Isak Dinesen

The twin yin forces of water over water create double danger. When the *I Ching* was written, the Chinese were agrarian rather than seafaring people. Thus they always equated the sea with danger and difficulty. This hexagram is also called Darkness, Abyss, or Abysmal. Sometimes the symbol is of a person falling into a pit. With such connotations, exercise care in everything you do. But also note that even if you fall, all is not lost. There is reason to hope, especially if you keep your wits about you.

There is no quick fix or easy answer for this situation. You also cannot hide from it, and must face facts and consequences. No matter what happens, remain calm. Courage, concentration, tenacity, and taking risks are called for now. In this hexagram you're reminded that danger comes for a reason and that connecting to your spirituality will strengthen you.

There are several valuable lessons to be learned. Trauma or tragedies do not break you; your reactions to them do. You have an opportunity to rise to the challenge with honesty and bravery. If you act appropriately and don't fall apart under pressure, the insights gained, peace of mind, and respect of others will be helpful for whatever comes after.

Fiction Question:

Most people claim that they embrace change, but in reality, most of us avoid change, danger, and conflict whenever possible. Yet when reading fiction, we read about people who are undergoing extreme changes and struggling and miserable for much of the story. And interestingly, the best parts of fiction are when the character is in the most trouble.

When you think about it, this practice of avoiding misery in life but pursuing it on the page is odd, but fiction aims to make readers uncomfortable. This discomfort is amplified by means of tension and suspense. Amid the character's sorrows and challenges we immerse ourselves in a life that's more difficult, dangerous, and interesting than our own. If you have selected this hexagram, examine each scene to determine if you have somehow made your character uncomfortable by creating small tensions in his environment or through dialogue. Notice too if you can use foreshadowing to suggest problems or dangers to come, since foreshadowing both adds credibility to future events but also causes fiction to whisper with tension.

Besides the more subtle aspects of scenes, ascertain whether each scene has enough conflict in the form of obstacles, roadblocks, and people trying to thwart your protagonist's scene goals.

Nonfiction Question:

In an interview, Scott Russell Sanders said:

The *contrasts* and *tensions* arise from my life—North/South, country and city, militarism and pacifism. Living as a boy in an arsenal in Ohio, I felt a fierce contrast between the fruitfulness and wildness of nature, on one hand, and the ingenuity and destructiveness of technology, on the other... As I write I keep seeing these contrasts ... and maybe I'm still trying to bring the two poles together, to reconcile enemies.

Record all the contrasts and tensions that you've experienced throughout your lifetime. Perhaps you're the only liberal in an office of conservatives, a Jew among Christians, a single woman among married friends with children. Perhaps you were the quiet one in a raucous family, a reader among a family of athletes, or a vegetarian among carnivores. Amid these tensions and contrasts, find inspiration.

The Writer's Path:

The writer's path requires tenacity, but that is especially true when trouble or trauma strikes. When tragedy must be coped with, it usually takes all of our resources to respond to the situation. Sometimes we're too depleted by grief or illness to accomplish more than the basic tasks of living.

Yet in the midst of trouble, never forget that you're a writer. Ask yourself not only what you can learn from the situation, but also make notes on your reactions, emotions, and grief. It is when you are most raw, exposed, and vulnerable that you are revealed. Over time these feelings ease, so you cannot always recall the depth of your anguish. This is the time to write for your eyes only: to express the situation in all its pain and rage. Everything in a writer's life is a gift, and when you can view trouble as material for writing, it is more bearable.

———

30. Shedding Light: Fire/Fire

The writer is always tricking the reader into listening to their dream.

—Joan Didion

It is as if the sun, moon, and stars are all providing illumination and radiance. This hexagram, with fire over fire, describes a time of synergy, optimism, and alignment. In fact, it is so hopeful that it is sometimes called Flaming Beauty or Brightness. Under this new and renewing light, remove the blinders and see your work and circumstances with clarity.

The light that shines now will distinguish right from wrong and the

———

appropriate from the inappropriate. If an opportunity for a partnership or joint effort appears, the project will likely succeed. It's also a time in which you can reorder relationships and negotiate partnerships for the best interests of both parties. If you encounter disagreements now, don't take them personally. Instead, operate from insight and detached awareness.

Align yourself with positive forces in the cosmos and within the self. Proceed at full speed when energies are high, but don't waste energy on an obsessive or frantic pace. When energies ebb, don't force yourself to keep plodding along. Instead, rest, read, plan, and gather your strength for your next assault.

Fiction Question:

Fictional plots fail for many reasons, but one of the chief reasons stems from the writer's failure to plan a story before he starts writing. It is especially difficult to write a novel if you don't know the ending. Knowing your ultimate destination helps in all aspects of plotting, but especially as you weave in foreshadowing.

Foreshadowing is a series of hints and whispers that set up events in the middle and final scenes. Like many fiction techniques it requires a delicate touch, but it also requires knowledge of where the story is headed. You want your reader to be surprised by the ending as well as the reversals layered throughout, but surprises only work when they are plausible. Lay the groundwork so that major events are believable. Foreshadowing not only hints at or plants information about later events, but helps continuity and deepens the sense of anticipation.

When and how much to foreshadow is a balancing act—too much and you defuse suspense; not enough and the story falls flat. Foreshadowing inserts a question or uneasiness in the reader's mind. These questions are not blatant but exist as underlying tension. Foreshadowing is usually woven into quieter moments, in dialogue and scene or chapter endings.

Nonfiction Question:

The best nonfiction illuminates what it means to be human amid a complicated, spinning world. Use your writing to shed light, because this is how change happens and understanding is created. But shedding light must be handled with intelligence and an open mind. People are never enlightened by a person who writes strictly from an agenda, emotions, or anger.

So how do you inspire readers with your life stories? You find truths and insights in small moments and everyday treasures. If the reader finds real people acting in real ways, he won't feel lectured to. Readers gain insights when universal themes are depicted, but universality is created through specific examples.

One method is to use anecdotes— stories within stories—to accomplish several aims. Anecdotes illuminate themes and truths. Themes work best when they're dramatized, not reported, so as these mini-stories unfold, ideas are delivered in sensory and gentle ways. Second, you're portraying people doing ordinary or extraordinary things, and these actions often serve as a microcosm for larger concepts. Third, anecdotes are a succinct way to reveal information in an engaging and often informal way. Finally, anecdotes deliver the more difficult aspects of life in a palatable dose. For example, if you're writing about the death of a child or parent, a single poignant moment at the funeral or a specific memory that illustrates what this person meant to the writer will speak volumes.

The Writer's Path:

Shedding Light reminds us how quickly time passes. For a person with writing goals, time can seem like the enemy because there is never enough. We all live within the reality of the twenty-four-hour cycle and the dictates of the calendar. If you allow a day to pass without writing, too soon it can become a week, a month, or a year. Annie Dillard wrote in *The Writing Life*, "How we spend our days is, of course, how we spend our lives." Think about this.

Dillard goes on to suggest that writers create a schedule for writing. She says:

> A schedule protects against chaos and whim. It is a net for catching days. It is a scaffolding on which a worker can stand and labor with both hands at sections of time. A schedule is a mock-up of reason and order—willed, faked, and so brought into being; it is a peace and a haven set into the wreck of time; it is a lifeboat on which you find yourself, decades later, still living.

So carve out time for writing day after day, week after week, month after month. If you don't, time will pass, and you'll wake months later as if from a daydream, merely older with a lingering sorrow about the opportunities missed.

—

31. Mutual Attraction: Lake/Mountain

Writing, at its best, is a lonely life. Organizations for writers palliate the writer's loneliness, but I doubt if they improve his writing. He grows in public stature as he sheds his loneliness and often his work deteriorates. For he does his work alone and if he is a good enough writer he must face eternity, or the lack of it, each day.

—Ernest Hemingway

Lake over mountain means that the mountain provides a foundation for the lake, while the lake provides water to nourish the mountain. This portrays good fortune and indicates that the time is right for lasting partnerships. Mutual

Attraction doesn't refer strictly to romance, but means forming a connection that will benefit both parties. If this is a business relationship, friendship, or family connection, remember that relationships require nurturing and consideration. Mutual Attraction warns not to impose your will, but instead to create partnerships based on trust and respect. Listen to what others can teach you now.

Look for true relationships, not flings or draining friendships. Approach people without prejudice, and appreciate each person's individuality. In these friendships and partnerships you should be yourself—relaxed, honest, and sincere. Your authenticity will attract like-minded people.

If you are struggling within a relationship, pay attention to the other person's values. Writers need kindred spirits to hold them up during the lonely hours of creating words on a page. Find yours.

Fiction Question:

Writing about love means that you are describing the indescribable, transporting the reader into a world built for two. Romantic love is one of the great mysteries of humanity—how two people connect has been the subject of endless conjecture and art over the centuries.

Since attraction is a mysterious business, depict a couple falling in love as if they have invented it. It requires a fresh approach, precise details, and a tightrope walk where the writer teeters between disclosure and withholding.

In lovemaking scenes, your reader wants to savor the intimate moments, the wildness, tenderness, and surrender, the primal drive, and the special sizzle of chemistry. Read widely in a variety of genres, noting what works and what doesn't. Keep in mind that you're trying to describe the *effects* of their passion, along with the conflict and tension that led up to it. Passion is never clinical, never melodramatic. It is always visual and sensory, giving the reader clear information about who is where in the scene.

Nonfiction Question:

We go through life analyzing the how and why of falling in and out of love. It is in matters of the heart that people are exposed as vulnerable and are most alive. But transforming this musing onto the page is no easy matter. Each person is uniquely complicated, and each relationship is a web of passions, adjustments, negotiations, and disappointments.

Try to find the significance in your relationships, past and present. Search for ways they are unique, satisfying, or troubling. Can you connect love to metaphors or analogies as a way to layer it with meaning? Can you spot family threads or legacies in how you love or fear to love? Capture the language of relationships using special words, pet names, or symbols. Dialogue captures the essence of two people together, as do the small moments when the truth of who they are is revealed.

The Writer's Path:

Often beginning writers need comrades for feedback and sustenance, friendship and sympathy. Joining a critique group can be either a huge boost or a detriment to your writing career. The trick is to choose wisely. Before joining, it's important to assess the members and interactions of the group. Are they ambitious go-getters? Or do they talk more about writing than actually doing it? Do the members regularly and promptly show up with new material—or with excuses for why they haven't written?

Evaluate your comfort level with the group. Most of us are nervous or afraid when we submit work for feedback. It's important to discern if your reactions are normal or if they're caused by the group's dynamics. Pay attention to the tone of feedback. If the feedback is catty, scathing, or personal, you're in the wrong group. In the best critique groups, the members are able to point out failings while giving specific information for correcting them and encouragement to try.

---

32. Perseverance: Thunder/Wind

When I sit at my table to write, I never know what it's going to be until I'm under way. I trust in inspiration, which sometimes comes and sometimes doesn't. But I don't sit back waiting for it. I work every day.

—Alberto Moravia

The wind has a gentle influence, while thunder stands for activity and strength. Favorable aspects are at play now and there is compatibility, as in a long-lasting marriage. If you are working on a meaningful project and are involved with the right people, a period of harmony lies ahead. Do not take things for granted because distractions are probably nagging at you. If you can ignore distractions and keep pushing toward your goals, you'll find success.

Persist and keep writing, no matter your mood or circumstances. Use your writing routine as a buffer against times when you bog down. It's not the proper time for a radical new approach or a shift in direction. Plodding determination and a traditional approach are called for. If a relationship or writing project is faltering, don't despair, because with patience and care you can right the situation. Be flexible when it comes to solutions and listen to others' opinions. Perseverance is another reminder to never overreact, no matter the provocation. Remember three things: commit, commit, commit.

Fiction Question:

When plotting fiction, keep in mind that everything in fiction is connected, every action is somehow linked. While real life can be random and unpredictable, randomness in fiction creates a chaotic and disconnected world that will disenchant and confuse readers.

Thus, when you're creating events, reactions, and motivations, you're always gazing into the future to see how these things will influence and drive the story. When causality is the connecting thread in fiction, it's easier to plan ramifications and generally create a cohesive world. One easy method of inserting causality is to make sure that every time a character makes a choice or decision, consequences—both good and bad—result.

Nonfiction Question:

Perseverance and all things connected to it are themes suited to essays and memoirs. The range of topics is endless. You can write about how you endured during a serious illness or caring for a sick person. You can write how you survived loss. Or you can write about an enduring love for chocolate. Or how you endured while running a marathon. Or how a tender memory of a certain event lingers with enduring poignancy.

Perseverance is a trait that doesn't receive much attention, yet it is something that you nurture in yourself and try to find in a mate. There is nothing as comforting as the person who stays at your side through good times and bad. Faithfulness and staying power are powerful themes for writing.

The Writer's Path:

Perseverance is perhaps the trait most needed by writers. It means writing when you feel like loafing, writing when you're low on inspiration, writing after a rejection or a setback. The ability to endure boredom, despair, and loneliness are core writing attributes.

Most of us come to writing in the midst of a busy life. True, some people have fewer responsibilities than others, but all writers must take that first step, then another, toward the computer. And once seated at the computer, they need endurance to stay there.

Nurturing your perseverance is also a matter of common sense. There will rarely be a perfect day or moment for writing. Often, it is the last thing you want to do, especially when your mood is wilted or defeated. But the only way to become a writer is to write through these moods and lulls, to walk toward words when you most want to run from them.

---

33. Retreat: Heaven/Mountain

I love to be alone. I never found the companion that was so companionable
as solitude. We are for the most part more lonely
when we go abroad among men than when we stay in our chambers.
A man thinking or working is always alone, let him be where he will.
Solitude is not measured by the miles of space
that intervene between a man and his fellows.
The really diligent student in one of the crowded hives
of Cambridge College is as solitary as a dervish in the desert.
            —Henry David Thoreau, *Walden*

The advice in Retreating is simple: step back and assess the situation. Imagine winter as the analogy of the hexagram. During the long months of cold, the earth rests, preparing for the garish blossoming of spring blooms.

This sort of retreat is not the same as running away or avoidance. Instead, it's part of a larger plan: a strategic move to maximize your position; a time to carefully judge your situation and make careful calculations.

Don't waste time on futile efforts, a frivolous lifestyle, or negative people. Conserve your energy for the work at hand. This hexagram reminds you that timing can be everything and confrontations can weaken, rather than strengthen, your position. Remember that retreat can be an honorable course in some situations, but it must be executed so that your self-respect is intact.

Fiction Question:

Backstory is a term that encompasses events and influences that happened before the story begins. Without a history, a plot and characters are thin and underdeveloped.

Like many fiction techniques, backstory requires finesse. As you write fiction, you'll accumulate lots of information about your characters. But this causes problems because the reader doesn't need to know everything that the writer knows. So you'll choose what to include and what to leave out. When making selections about backstory information, remember that it must shine a light of significance onto the front story, or events moving forward. It cannot be a random smattering of details, a catalogue of events or memories. The history must matter and if possible, cause ramifications.

Backstory also explains the milieu of the story world and provides character motivation. It reveals what is at stake if the protagonist wins or loses. For example, in a mystery, the reader rarely witnesses the murder, so backstory will provide the who, how, and why of the crime. The reader will come to care that the victim was murdered, intrigued by the events that led to the murder and the people the victim was entangled with, and then will want the detective to solve the crime. In a romance, backstory informs us of the important events and influences in the hero and heroine's pasts that serve to keep them apart or thwart their easy acquiescence in love.

Nonfiction Question:

The landscape of childhood is filled with memory and sweetness. It includes rituals such as the first and last day of school, holidays, birthdays, and

Easter morning. Along with rituals, you recall the everyday world, the bedrooms, classrooms, kitchens, and backyards of childhood. Travel back in time and find the people from your past, including favorite uncles and teachers as well as neighborhood bullies and older kids you looked up to. Explore how the place you came from shaped you. Recall your childhood influences and trace how they still influence you now.

There is a larger reason for writing about the past—it is because childhood memories unleash the writer within. June Gould in *The Writer in All of Us* explains:

> Childhood memories build the foundation for creative and imaginative writing. Memories and our power to imagine are intertwined. When we remember, our image-making power is released, and our writing becomes creative, imaginative, and delightful.

Another important reason for remembering your past is that your memories come to you with the senses intertwined—fresh mown grass, the chalky smell of a classroom, your grandmother's kitchen, the sounds of rain on the roof as you drifted off to sleep in your childhood bed. And writing for the senses is the foundation of a writing practice. Gould writes:

> Making the decision to start remembering will lower a long fishing line into the depths of your past. Once you have decided to write, you will be surprised at how many memories start tugging at you. The whole world—nature, family, books, TV, news, movies, conversation—will seem to exist solely to remind you of your childhood.

The Writer's Path:

Sometimes the best approach to the writing life is to retreat and recharge your creative batteries. However, this approach must be handled with care. Writers avoid writing when a project isn't going well, and sometimes even when it's going smoothly. So you must discern when you're truly weary and empty of inspiration. When it is clear that you're in a slump, you must consciously give yourself permission to take a break to renew yourself.

Perhaps you need to slip out of town for a few days. Maybe you need to watch movies, read books, or cook large quantities of your favorite foods. Whatever means you choose for renewal, it should soothe, nurture, and replenish. Your off time also needs a clear deadline because *not* writing can be amazingly seductive. Don't abandon your project and then allow days to pass before you return to it. Two or three days off are usually enough for a recharge. Another warning here: this is not a time for socializing or partying. Retreat and reflect.

34. Great Strength: Thunder/Heaven

Originality and a feeling of one's own dignity
are achieved only
through work and struggle.

—Fyodor Dostoyevsky

Thunder is rolling through the heavens and the rain that follows will nurture the earth below. But severe storms can cause problems such as flooding or mudslides. In the same fashion, harsh means can cause problems in your life. You have the opportunity to profoundly impact a situation now, but you must exercise care. Use diplomacy and planning in all you do. While an opportunity for influence exists, don't throw your weight around or flaunt your strength.

Instead, Great Strength means that you make decisions based on what is good for all, that you consider advice, and that you take action based on solid plans. Imagine how a diplomat negotiates treaties: he knows that success comes from patience and tact, not manipulation and tantrums. If you play the bully, the results will haunt you.

It's an important time to focus and act accordingly. If you are tempted to flout the rules, this hexagram warns that disaster will result.

Fiction Question:

In fiction the protagonist is the main character whom the reader follows and develops empathy for. He's the star and has the burden of carrying many of the story's emotions. Readers are drawn to people who are likeable and self-actualized, and who set out to achieve their goals. The protagonist typically exists to reveal the themes the author wants to express.

A hero is a sub-category of protagonist, but a hero has something more; he is trustworthy because we come to know his values, capabilities, and focus. He often works as a champion for society, and when he is introduced, the reader immediately sympathizes and empathizes with him, cheering for him during his struggles and battles. His goal in the story—slay the dragon, hunt down the killer, right a wrong—is to serve the good of all.

While fictional characters are larger than life, a hero is brazenly large. Heroes often possess qualities that we admire, beyond bravery or the willingness to sacrifice the self. They can also be steadfast in love or in danger, willing to overcome flaws, willing to look foolish or weak if it's called for, able to see the big picture when others cannot, or ask hard questions that others will not. In other words, heroic qualities come in many shades.

Nonfiction Question:

Personal essays are powerful means to tell a story, state an opinion, or explore a topic. In an essay, the writer is the source of the material. Essays are more intimate and less formal than journalism, shorter than memoir. The subject can be large or small, but it requires the writer to take an emotional risk. Since he writes to evoke emotions in the reader, he also displays his own emotions in the process.

Essayists don't need to be objective; in fact, being opinionated is a great asset. Essays are written in a natural and conversational style, with a voice similar to the one the writer uses while chatting and drinking coffee with a friend. Punctuated with anecdotes and perhaps bits of dialogue, the style will depend on the needs of the subject. Some subjects will demand a serious tone; others will work if the tone is flippant, wry, or silly.

Keep in mind that essays often seem to cover a small subject—birds in a winter garden—but then, as the subject is explored, the essay ventures into larger themes. In this case, perhaps the essayist is writing about hope, resiliency, or the cycles of things. These deeper meanings can have profound implications and create deep layers of understanding.

The Writer's Path:

Learning to give balanced and fair feedback is an important skill on the writing path. Many of us feel exposed and uneasy when our work is read. And strangely, those same feelings hold when we read someone else's words. After all, who are we to offer advice?

In the critique process, both sides can win. The reader wins because critical reading sharpens his editing and proofreading skills. Here are tips for giving feedback to a fellow writer:

1. Remember that your purpose in critiquing is to provide support

and illuminating analysis. Thus, begin your critique with at least one positive statement about the writer's strengths.

2. If you see room for improvement, make specific suggestions. For example, if the writer has relied on clichés, too much telling and not enough showing, or sloppy transitions, point out these issues.

3. Guard against sounding condescending, sarcastic, or cranky. If you cannot offer an upbeat, affirming tone, avoid commenting.

4. End your feedback with another positive statement. For example, "I'd love to read more of your work because I'm hooked on your characters." Or, "I liked your voice; the word choices, metaphors, and dialogue were rich and vivid."

Remember that you are critiquing the writing, not the writer. Respect the work. This is not your writing and you should not attempt to overhaul the work as if it were. Consider the stage of the work. If it's an early draft, focus your comments on content. If it's a "final" ready for submission, provide a more in-depth analysis.

———

35. Progress: Fire/Earth

We have to continually be jumping off cliffs and developing our wings on the way down.

—Kurt Vonnegut

Fire, which symbolizes the sun, is shining brightly on the earth below. Full speed ahead! In fact, things might be moving faster than you ever dared imagine. Your strengths have paid off, your ideas are appreciated, and recognition is possible. Traditional portrayals of this hexagram were of a benevolent prince giving away horses and receiving horses from his subjects.

———

Under these auspices, make certain that you are also acting with generosity and clarity. It is time to both give and receive recognition, praise, and rewards. However, your methods of communicating are important, so fine-tune your approach. Make sure that you're understood, sincere, and truthful.

If you need to re-invent yourself or choose a new writing direction, this is a great time to switch. If you need to promote yourself or approach people in positions of power, your timing is perfect. When this hexagram is chosen, it is time to reflect on your inner world and make adjustments. Progress is also a time when you can establish a lasting foundation for your writing career.

Fiction Question:

A hook refers to the opening that compels a reader to keep reading. The hook piques curiosity, sets the tone, focuses attention, and establishes voice. Your opening also indicates overall pacing and makes promises to a reader about what type of story you're telling. A hook can be a single sentence or a whole chapter. A hook is not a gimmick, even though you're often teasing the reader with what is to come.

A reader wants to feel as if he has landed in the story and can unpack his suitcase and immediately wander around in this world. Thus, the opening uses details to provide a map of sorts. Make certain that the reader is aware of the time of day, season, climate, and general geographic location as the story opens.

The reader's first glimpse of the narrator, story world, and characters should be unforgettable. Avoid details that don't get the story off the ground, such as spending time inside a character's thoughts: plunge in with action.

Another aspect of the hook is that it introduces, or hints at, conflict and the story question. Sometimes a hook raises a question that needs answering, In fact, most stories contain at least one central question teasing the reader. In *To Kill A Mockingbird,* one question in the story is who is the real Boo Radley and why does he hide from the world? And why does he leave the children presents? From the opening pages the recluse ignites the imaginations of Scout, Jem and Dill and hooks the reader with questions. In a suspense novel the question that is often introduced fairly early in the story is who committed a murder and why. Readers also wonder how the victim knew the murderer and if he or she represented some kind of threat. In a romance novel, once the hero and heroine meet, the question is: will they overcome their obstacles to love? If your hook raises a question, the reader will continue reading, longing for an answer.

Nonfiction Question:

The lead or opening in nonfiction has two main jobs to accomplish: to make readers care and to prove the writer's credibility. But this must be done quickly, so the lead is multitasking in only a few sentences. The best openings convince the reader to read further, promising that what comes next will bring meaning to his life. Openings must also announce the tone or mood of the piece. Tone can vary widely: wry, silly, thoughtful, or caustic. But while openings must be engaging, they are not contrived, melodramatic, or forced. Instead, a well-crafted opening is specific, original, and engaging. It convinces the reader that the writer can handle the task at hand.

A good opening pushes ahead, and doesn't let the reader stop to ponder what has just been said. Often, the best nonfiction openings borrow from fictional or narrative techniques. You can begin with a direct or offbeat quote, an anecdote, description, or an action. You can also begin with paraphrasing or an indirect quote.

Don't always begin at the beginning. You might want to start your piece midway, and then circle back to opening events. Think about how plays and movies begin—the action dives in immediately, not with a character on stage introducing what is about to come. Consider also using a structure that opens with a mystery and then unfolds to solve it.

The Writer's Path:

In the publishing world, there are rules that you can bend and then there are those that are nonnegotiable. Here is one that you can take to the bank: your manuscript's first impression is crucial and must sparkle with professionalism. If your manuscript *looks* like it was sent by an amateur, it will likely be ignored. If for some reason an editor is *forced* to read your flawed manuscript, your formatting mistakes will cast a shadow over the content.

Editors and agents complain that amateurs do not have the courtesy to follow basic guidelines such as properly numbering pages, double spacing, or inserting a slug line.

Send only crisp copies, never dog-eared ones. Don't print on colored paper or in a font smaller than 12 points. Find a good resource on manuscript submissions or ask the publisher for its specifications. When you approach a pro, follow the rules.

36. Laying Low: Earth/Fire

To be out of harmony with one's surroundings is of course a misfortune,
but it is not always a misfortune to be avoided at all costs.
Where the environment is stupid or prejudiced or cruel,
it is a sign of merit to be out of harmony with it.

—Bertrand Russell

The structure of Laying Low portrays a setting sun, which indicates adversity. Keep a low profile and bide your time, because hostility exists or enemies are about. You are in a period in which you may need to hide your intelligence and knowledge for your own protection. You might also need to disguise your talents or true feelings.

It is unwise to assert yourself, so find other means to remain true to your convictions.

Laying Low can also refer to working at a task that is beneath you. It is possible that a project is more difficult than you anticipated and involves drudgery. Keep at it anyway, and keep your opinions to yourself. In the end, you'll profit from diligence and self-control.

If you're feeling lonely or excluded, this is only a passing phase. Know yourself and don't allow anyone to sway you from your path. Avoid confrontations, bide your time, and bury yourself in work. Use this time wisely; focus on your inner world and work rather than socializing. Eventually this period will end and you'll emerge victorious.

Fiction Question:

While scenes are about goals and excitement, the sequel or follow-up to a scene is based on feeling and logic. The sequel is where your character responds emotionally and intellectually to the previous scene. The sequel also provides the transition between two scenes.

The three elements of a sequel are reaction, dilemma, and decision. Often, when a dramatic event happens in real life, our first reactions are emotional. We lash out, weep, lose our temper, or give in to despair or humiliation. Before we can think through what has happened, we first experience raw feelings.

In fiction, after the character stops reeling emotionally he starts trying to solve the problem. He analyzes what has just happened, mulls over the dilemma it presents, ponders his next actions, and then reaches a decision. And then, because fiction is causal and forward moving, he plans his next action.

Not every scene will be followed by a sequel followed by another scene. Sequels occur as a means of pacing, inserting information, and deepening characterization. Sequels also most often follow highly-charged events and especially traumatic events. The pattern you develop for scene and sequel will depend on the needs of the overall structure. Another tip to remember is that you can sometimes slip a flashback into a sequel because if it was inserted into the scene, it would dilute the drama. The amount of sequel contained in a plot also depends on the genre. Romance novels have more sequels than action novels because they focus on the characters' emotions and inner life, while action plots are woven around scenes.

Nonfiction Question:

Nonfiction requires details that stir the reader's emotions and anchor the writing, yet these details must possess emotional significance for the person noticing them. Details bring nonfiction to life, but they must be selected with extreme care. For example, your readers will feel rooted in your memoir because you've included specific information about the setting. But these are not just *any* details.

Reveal details that capture the *essence* and *mood* of the place. Try inserting music, or some other means of reflecting an era, into the moment. Perhaps your details will indicate the time of year by using features of a garden or elements of nature; these indicators can also stand for an emotional context. A garden in spring can connote hope or a fresh start, while a garden that is overrun from neglect expresses another idea.

Specificity is easy to overdo. Don't overload the story with sensory assault, a catalogue, or a list. Find distinctive sensory impressions that you can slip into the story—smells, sounds, textures—then render them evocatively. But be selective. A single scent, such as cinnamon or lilac or jasmine, can become a sort of sensory shorthand that connects the reader with a complex idea or place.

The Writer's Path:

When you receive a critique, here a few things to remember: Criticism is necessary for growth and improvement. It is sometimes difficult not to take criticism personally, but it is important to understand that it is part of the learning process. Don't allow criticism to discourage you from putting your ideas out there.

View a critique of your work as an opportunity. Avoid extreme reactions such as "I am right, thus the other person is wrong." Remember that you are free to disagree with a critique. However, make the effort to understand the feedback first before you draw conclusions about its validity.

Before you submit a piece to be critiqued, determine if it is appropriate for the class or group format. While a critique group or writing class exists to provide support for each member's writing, support does not equal therapy. If the piece is too personal, controversial, or difficult to reveal to the group, don't present it. If you need feedback on a particularly sensitive topic, you can show it to a trusted friend instead.

Make the process easier by being specific about what you hope to gain from the critique. Respect the process. Submit work that has been proofread, since a draft riddled with spelling errors and typos distracts from the quality of the writing.

Avoid defending yourself and your work. Keep an open mind and listen without response when appropriate. If someone critiques in a way that you don't understand, ask for clarification, but don't argue. Graciously thank the group for their feedback, even if you don't agree with it.

Trust your instincts. Before altering anything based on another writer's comments, take time to absorb the feedback. If the suggestions strengthen the work, keep them. If not, try a fresh approach that still accommodates the suggestions. Realize that only you, the writer, hold the vision of your piece.

37. The Family: Wind/Fire

There is no pleasure in the world like writing well and going fast.
—Tennessee Williams

In traditional drawings of this hexagram, a roof was drawn over a valuable domesticated animal, indicating the importance of family. The Family is also influenced by the yang energy of wind and fire that can whip up a raging firestorm in an instant. Since yang energies have potential for good or harm, they must be tamed.

All concerns about family and your environment are highlighted. The Family does not refer strictly to a traditional family but can also mean partnerships, relationships, and the writing community. This hexagram reminds you that while isolation is necessary for writing, support and nurturing from others keep you going. For now, avoid spending too much time alone and seek cooperation and the company of others.

The Family also reminds you to nurture relationships with consideration, compassion, and integrity. If there are problems in your family or business, address them with firmness and an open mind. If any role in the group is out of sync, make adjustments. View all relationships as you would a family; act with warmth, and especially with loyalty and consistency.

Fiction Question:

Creating a crowd scene presents challenges for most writers. In films, as the camera pans among the crowd, we listen in on conversations and watch characters reacting to each other. Robert Altman's *Gosford Park* features mostly group scenes, many chronicling the "upstairs-downstairs" dynamic between the English upper class and working class. In fiction, a crowd scene is harder to create because the reader cannot keep hopping around a room or delving into more than one character's thoughts within a scene.

Your first step is to determine the scene's purpose. How many characters are needed to portray the action? Sometimes beginning writers believe that they need a crowd when a few interesting people are enough; overpopulating the scene dilutes the action.

Next, determine which point of view will serve as the filter for the scene. If your novel has a single viewpoint, your decision is easy. If you've created multiple points of view, it is still necessary to stick with one per scene and avoid head-hopping.

Janet Evanovich's Stephanie Plum series often depicts crowd scenes, most of them occurring around the family dinner table. Plum often ends up at her mother's New Jersey home at dinner time, lured by fried chicken or pot roast, pineapple upside-down cake, and other goodies. As the series has progressed, the crowd around the table has grown: Her sister has moved back home with her daughters; her sister's fiancé and Plum's boyfriend often join the meal; her batty grandmother cracks one-liners; and her father steadfastly busies himself with his mashed potatoes.

The key to the success of these scenes is that the scene is delivered from a single viewpoint, and the reader is anchored in reality by the snappy dialogue along with meat loaf, chocolate cake, and homey smells. And readers have also come to know the characters better with each book in the series. Evanovich is also careful to use terse dialogue and insert humor to keep us riveted to the event.

The second key to creating a crowd scene is to add an element of tension; usually during these meals, Plum is trying to hide some danger from her family as her father reacts to the strange family dynamics and her mother tries to ferret out the truth.

Nonfiction Question:

For nonfiction writers, the family is the nest that we never leave. In our musing about family and sometimes in a desperate search to understand our own families, we find fascinating topics for exploration. These realms appeal to readers, who also spend a lifetime sorting out the contradictions, pains, and blessings of families.

In *Long Quiet Highway*, Natalie Goldberg writes about how she was shaped by her family and a suburban existence on Long Island. It was a world of safety, with her grandparents sleeping in the next room, but also of dullness and limitation. Goldberg began looking for authors who offered role models as an antidote. She writes, "I was looking for the salve for my personal grief... I needed these people, because I came from different but similar American beginnings. Loneliness and alienation were my dead center inheritance."

It took her years to recognize this inheritance, find herself within this milieu, and understand her family influences. This journey began in earnest when she left home to attend college and turned to writing.

> When I became a writer and wrote my first furtive poem at twenty-four years old, I was free. Suddenly the cramped quarters in our split-level at 50 Miller Road became big, an arena to explore, and I did not have to wrestle with anyone else's desires. No one in my family had ever dreamed of being a writer. This turned out to be a great gift.

Tell readers what you have learned about legacy and family. Wrap your understanding amid the many contradictions, sorrows, and splendors that shaped you.

The Writer's Path:

A current trend involves writing instant books and e-books to make a quick profit. The author researches a subject and, like a ghostwriter, pens a book with the bottom line strictly in mind. And for some people this works because writing is a job, just as being an accountant is a job.

But if you have chosen this hexagram for guidance, write not only what you want to read, but also what you care deeply about. If you write only for the marketplace, your lack of sincerity will be revealed. Instead, write what draws you as to a fire on a cold night, what kindles your passions and obsessions. Consider how in The Family, the wind is fed by the fire of family love.

Write what you love, and choose topics that echo with personal meaning. Be sincere in how you approach your career and this will benefit everything you attempt.

38. Opposition: Fire/Lake

In the dark time, the eye begins to see.

—Theodore Roethke

The original translation of this hexagram was "Eyes do not look at each other." Since fire extends upward and the lake descends downward, situations can deteriorate. People see things differently, and while this causes difficulty it also adds diversity to a situation. Opposition and contradictions can take many forms now.

If you are in the midst of a serious disagreement or a difficult negotiation, listen to differing viewpoints and opinions. Weigh other people's words carefully before answering. There is a strong possibility of misunderstandings and serious rifts, so settle matters creatively and carefully. Respect differing points of view and be adaptable.

Opposition can also provide opportunity. If you can work through your disagreements with another person, your relationship or project can be revived. There is also a deeper issue here—life is full of opposition and contradictions, and it's necessary to learn how to cope with this reality. The world is made of opposites such as fire and water, and it is time to work within this understanding rather than fight it.

Finally, duality and contradictions lie within each of us. This hexagram reminds you to accept the many parts of self and find ways to make peace with your nature and opposing desires. Don't struggle to overcome duality, but instead understand that it makes you unique and strengthens your outlook and personality.

Fiction Question:

While many stories feature a protagonist plagued by outer conflict such as an antagonist, physical danger, or nature unleashing its horrors, internal conflict is another element of storytelling. Internal conflict forces your character to make difficult choices, take risks, and ultimately change. Inner conflict must also be externalized or dramatized in some fashion. When not handled carefully, inner conflict can be static, or depict a character who seems self-involved.

If you analyze most fiction, you realize that the best stories blend inner and outer conflict, one playing off the other. But how do you introduce inner conflict that gnaws at your character? First, the internal conflict cannot be a single, one-time quandary. It is layered into the character's psyche and the unfolding events of the story. The story must keep circling around it while outside pressures demand release.

Second, most events and complications are designed to throw your character off balance. And a character who is out of balance is interesting and desperate. A character needs to be straining, grasping, and clinging to his sanity or wits through most of the story.

Another trick to creating inner conflict is to force a character to make tough choices that he would rather ignore, and link the choices to his emotional core. Give the character dilemmas that clash with his beliefs and values or provide some sort of test.

Nonfiction Question:

A crucial aspect of writing about your life is to present a balanced view. If you cannot see yourself honestly with all your flaws and strengths, understanding the role you have played in your own problems, your writing will be one-dimensional.

There is nothing quite as attractive as a person who can laugh at himself, admit his flaws and foibles, and admit his role in a disaster, even if it makes him look shallow or foolish. David Sedaris has made a career of mocking himself, following a long tradition of writers that includes Mark Twain, Truman Capote, and Dorothy Parker. Or think of Woody Allen's career, and the string of neurotic characters he creates and plays in his movies.

Revealing our flaws is a complicated issue. In *Writing from Personal Experience*, Nancy Davidoff Kelton explains that nonfiction writers must bring a willingness to share to the table. She writes, "To my mind, all good writing is self-revelatory. Which means letting others see your insides. This takes honesty, sincerity and courage."

What readers long for is the unexpected in revelations, but unexpected does not necessarily means salacious. We want to meet a writer who is not afraid of his mirror and can unmask himself, warts and all. But the writer doesn't need to be naked. Beginning writers often benefit from a class or critique group that helps them determine if their honesty works or is self-serving.

The Writer's Path:

While ambition is laudable and goals are necessary, shooting for the stars before you're ready spells doom for most beginning writers. Shooting for the stars means sending an article to a national magazine even though you have not been published yet. It means mailing your manuscript to agents although you've never taken a fiction class or worked in a critique group. This is like expecting that in a corporation you'll be promoted from the mailroom to the boardroom without any steps in between.

The stars exist to remind us of the constant wonder of this planet, to inspire us nightly with their jeweled display. But back on terra firm, pay your dues and establish your career one step at a time. Realistic goals are the ones that work in the long run as you build your skills, collect clips of your publishing credits, and learn from the editors whom you work with.

---

39. Obstacles: Water/Mountain

Mystery is not much in favor these days. The notion that there are limits
to what we can do, what we can know, limits to our dominion,
does not sell well with kings and queens of the hill. Humility and reverence,
we hear, are attitudes of cowards. Why worship a face we cannot measure
on a meter? Why tell stories about a power we cannot photograph?
—Scott Russell Sanders

The *I Ching* was written during centuries of war, political upheaval, and struggles for power in ancient China. Thus, many of its hexagrams warn of subterfuge and dangers. Hexagram 39 warns of possible difficulties, hardship, and obstacles. Like the previous hexagram, it also reminds us that hardship is a natural part of life. When you accept this truth, it's easier to deal with it.

Anticipate roadblocks and plan ahead. Do not allow adversity to throw you off balance. You are likely to be stuck on a project or in the midst of some difficulty and cannot yet see your way out, but don't despair. Quit struggling and miring yourself deeper in the situation. You need another approach or vision, and that might mean taking a break for a while so that you can see the situation anew. Step away, disengage, and consolidate your strength. If necessary, join others who offer solutions, leadership, and advice.

Another person or a group may represent your obstacle, but don't blame others. The real problems stem from your attitudes and anxiety, as well as an incorrect strategy. A new approach and vision can reinvigorate your whole world.

Fiction Question:

Fiction requires obstacles for a protagonist to overcome: obstacles that block his happiness. All scenes are built around conflict so that the reader never forgets its urgent, looming presence. However, while the conflict must be urgent, it also needs to be plausible and believable, simmering in varying degrees of intensity. In a mystery novel, evidence disappears; a witness is silenced or murdered. In a romance, an antagonist appears on the scene to thwart a blooming relationship.

Obstacles are generally not anticipated, so provide an extra sizzle when they thwart the protagonist: a terrible storm stalls the rescue; a lover from the heroine's past moves back to town; two men love the same woman or two women love the same man; supplies run out; a car breaks down as a dangerous storm looms; innocent people are in the way when the police are chasing the villain; the bridge is washed out; the truth cannot be revealed because it will destroy too many people.

Obstacles generate suspense because readers need a reason to worry. Often, in fiction there is the sense that the clock is ticking and time is running out, creating more tension. For example, if an issue is not solved in time, a patient will die, a criminal will go free, a storm will thunder through and knock out the power just as a delicate operation is scheduled, a killer will strike again, an innocent will be killed, or the truth will be revealed too late to save someone.

Obstacles comes in many forms—a tug of wills or pressures coming from someone, something, or nature. Readers must witness a struggle: an argument, a challenge, an exhausting journey, a search, a puzzle unfolding, a fistfight, a chase, an interrogation, a rumor run amok, or a showdown. Obstacles are also depicted as tests, and tests of all types force the reader to keep turning pages, fretting about the outcome.

Nonfiction Question:

It is commonly known that conflict is the engine that drives fiction, but it is rarely understood that conflict also often drives nonfiction. All stories, including essays, need an underlying impetus and intensity, and conflict creates that intensity. It sometimes reveals a writer grappling with fresh wounds or long-buried feelings pouring onto the page.

Topics for conflict are everywhere, but an easy place to begin is to make a list of all the things that you are not. Your mother is a Martha Stewart sort of person; you are not. Your husband lines up his tools with such precision that his workshop looks like a NASA laboratory, while your kitchen is a jumble.

Find the places in life where you struggle to better yourself or fight against your nature. Write about the conflicts that you've been muddling through in therapy, about how you never knew your father because he abandoned your family when you were five, or how you never fit in with the lifestyle of the suburbs. Write about how your best friend does not dare come out of the closet. Write about being a minister's wife when you were born to carouse.

As in fiction, conflict can also be found in the broader strokes of life, the larger themes. For example: Who am I and how does this differ from who I wish I was? How has my family or society shaped my values? How much am I willing to suffer to achieve my dreams? How do I live my values? What were my worst moments? What lessons did I learn the hard way?

The Writer's Path:

While it's important to pursue your writing goals, it's also important not to be a cruel taskmaster. If you've chosen this hexagram, this is a reminder to be a gentle guardian to your writer within.

It's so easy to castigate yourself, to see your faults and lacks, and to fret about how you never quite measure up. But one secret of the writing path is that the stories that live inside your imagination are always more vivid, interesting, and evocative than those that end up on the page. Your lifelong task is to steadily shrink the gap between the stories that you imagine and those that you actually write. To improve constantly, nudging yourself along as you would encourage a child learning how to ride a bicycle or how to swim. You don't badger a child into learning something scary; you coax, encourage, praise, and nurture. You cradle the child as he floats in the shallow end of the pool. You hold up the bicycle while voicing confidence, reassuring him that he's safe until he can venture out solo.

So build your skills step by step, improving, always improving. But don't expect too much of yourself. There will be good days of writing and bad days. Expect both, and be kind to yourself no matter the outcome of each day.

40. Release: Thunder/Water

Don't worry about what the world needs.
Ask what makes you come alive and do that.
Because what the world needs are people who have come alive.

—Howard Thurman

Thunder, swift and mighty, is pushing at the water below and the results are movement, progress, and positive influences. It's as if a wild storm has swept through, and afterward everything is washed clean and the danger is over. After the storm passes, energy is released, tension is diminished, and a fresh phase begins.

Release recommends that situations and problems must be addressed immediately with force, assertiveness, and resolve. But only if the timing is right. If a positive outcome can result, remove the obstacles in your path or deal with issues that emerge no matter what it takes. If a project is stalled, forge ahead and complete it. If the situation is too dangerous at this time, bypass it if possible and make headway along some other path..

Don't waste energy on emotional turmoil; resolve grievances without drama and move beyond past mistakes. Once you deal with problems, you'll notice new clarity and energy. But remember, don't procrastinate; act quickly, and then notice how open water lies ahead.

Release also speaks about handling emotional blockage, and suggests that you deal generously with difficult people. Once liberation occurs, return to your regular routines and carry on.

Fiction Question:

In fiction, falling action comes after the climax. In these final pages, complications are untangled and sorted out, tensions subside, and the story moves toward its conclusion. It contrasts sharply with the rising action in the events leading up to the climax. Here, the reader witnesses the consequences of the story's events.

As you write these final scenes, keep a few things in mind. First, don't linger too long on the falling action. Conclude the story as quickly as possible and get off the stage. Second, remember that the best endings linger in the reader's memory, so create a final moment, image, or dialogue exchange that delivers poignancy. Finally, as you are resolving tensions, make certain that you match the character's feelings to the actions in the climax. If your character has won the race, will he gloat? If your character has lost everything, will he be embittered, hold a grudge, or find a way to carry on?

By the time the reader has reached the falling action, he has witnessed a dramatic climax, so don't explain too much. The climax might be a physical fight, a verbal showdown, or a shift whereby the protagonist now has a new awareness. Often, in the falling action, the protagonist undergoes a reappraisal of all that has happened, especially the final events of the plot.

Nonfiction Question:

Twelve-step groups are famous for advising members to "just let go" or "let go and let God," while practitioners of Buddhism are advised to "let go and let be." This advice means surrendering control of a person, situation, behavior, or emotion because our need to control or cling has become destructive. Once this surrender takes place, relief and release supposedly follow.

Most of us are much more comfortable with control than surrender. And we discover that juxtaposed with the freedom of letting go are grieving and loss. First comes recognizing your need to surrender, then a decision to do so, followed by acceptance. Woven into the process are faith, trust, and a willingness to move in a healthier direction.

For most of us, the process is not easy, but like many places where growth and pain intersect, it is fruitful ground for writing nonfiction. Explore this topic by making a list of all the times that you let go. Perhaps you were engaged in a futile power struggle with your teenager, and realized that if you were to survive his teen years, you'd need to let go of some control and shift your expectations. Perhaps you learned to let go when someone you loved died. Perhaps you needed to let go of a friendship or relationship that you'd outgrown. Or maybe you let go of a bad habit or a destructive pattern in your relationships. Some must learn to let go of the past, emotional patterns such as depression or anger, or even long-held dreams. Whatever the issue, follow the process from entanglement to acceptance, showing the reader the power of surrender.

The Writer's Path:

It has been debated whether writer's block is real or neurosis. Some experts claim there is no such thing as writer's block, while others assert its reality. No matter which side you choose, it is important to understand the factors at work when you feel stalled. Sometimes when you believe that you're blocked, you're actually unprepared for the project that you're working on.

In *Page After Page*, author Heather Sellers confesses that she never believed in writer's block until it happened to her. She warns:

> It's important to make a distinction between a writing block, a
> nervous breakdown, fear of writing and the lack on knowing *how*
> to write. They are each different states.

If your life has been upended by a trauma, loss, or death in the family, it's likely that writing will be difficult. The same is true if you're moving, working sixty hours a week, recently gave birth to twins, or are battling a serious illness. All these things take energy and recovery time.

But if you arrive at your writing space blank and empty, day after day, you should suspect other factors at work. Learn all you can about the genre you're writing in. Read widely for inspiration and instruction. Find support for your dreams and answers to your lack of skills.

If you're truly blocked, you must outsmart your empty brain. Experiment, dabble, create a collage, or write limericks. Whatever it takes. You must find a way back to the joy of writing.

41. Low Tide: Mountain/Lake

The good ending dismisses us with a touch of ceremony, and throws a backward light of significance over the story just read. It makes it, as they say, or unmakes it, —a weak beginning is forgettable, but the end of a story bulks in the reader's mind like the giant foot in a foreshortened photograph.

—John Updike

As the mountain grows, the lake lowers because it turns into rain falling on the mountain. Applying this concept to your life, this means that to everything there is a season, and this one is about dwindling or waning forces. It's important to know how to handle situations when forces are in a decline. Instead of fighting the circumstances, set your priorities. If it's called for, simplify your routine or needs. If you meet losses or setbacks, respond with sincerity and redoubled efforts. No matter what happens during this phase, remain calm and confident. The cycle will swing back to increase, but first accept this phase.

If you typically dramatize situations or give in to anxiety, correct these behavior patterns. Notice your reactions to problems and modulate them. If you're involved in any emotionally draining relationships, slip away or refuse to become entangled in arguments. This is a good time for isolation, restraint, and focusing on your projects and peace of mind.

Fiction Question:

One of the most common problems that editors cite is that endings often fall short or somehow don't jell. Two problems are common: the ending is overdone, with the writer droning on and on, or it is too abrupt, and the reader leaves the story world feeling unsettled. The best fictional endings persist in the reader's imagination and provide a backward glance at the story, shining a spotlight on the previous events so the reader perceives them with new poignancy.

Remember that anything after the climax is anticlimactic, so it must be justified. Your ending will be determined by the story type; some can be quiet or thoughtful, but all must give the reader a last look of significance. In short stories the final words are especially crucial and sometimes writers use symbols, images, or metaphors rather than action to make meaning resonate.

Genre fiction, such as mystery or romance, tends to end on an upbeat or hopeful note. Nancy Kress, author of *Beginnings, Middles & Ends* advises, "This is your reader's last sound from the fictional world of your story. Don't waste the chance to choose carefully what the last sound should be: a whisper, a laugh, a bang, a whimper."

Nonfiction Question:

Essays require a structure: a hook that invites readers into the subject, a middle that develops the subject, and an ending that leaves the reader musing. The middle paragraphs provide the context and necessary data so that the message can be understood, and sometimes include weaving in statistics, background information, and quotes from experts.

An essay is focused on only a few key points. Essays fail when a writer veers too far afield, bringing in examples from widely divergent parts of life, or trying to encompass a dozen points within a thousand words.

Focusing on a single issue while making two or three key points usually works best. Apply this focus, and avoid mixed metaphors or complicated imagery. Often, the best essays are the simplest. In nonfiction, as in many types of writing, simplicity equals eloquence.

The Writer's Path:

One of the main tenets of Buddhism is that while life is difficult, suffering is optional. Life will always dole out woes and difficulties, but it is your reactions to trouble that define you and ultimately guarantee your happiness or misery.

Hexagram 41 is a powerful reminder that modulating your emotions and avoiding drama will help every aspect of your life, but especially your writing path. Develop strategies that will keep the drama on the stage or in the stories you're writing, not in your life.

Drama comes in many guises: mysterious illnesses, obsessive thoughts or behaviors, weird sleep patterns, invented dilemmas, and exaggerated tragedies. You need to use this energy in your work, not in your emotions.

It might also be helpful to post a reminder in your writing space about remaining emotionally grounded. It might be a statue of Buddha with his enigmatic smile, a few passages of scripture, or a quote from an artist you admire. But first comes facing facts: You are taking yourself too seriously. You've lost your sense of humor, and you are too self-absorbed. And whatever your spiritual affiliation, remember that suffering is optional.

—

42. High Tide: Wind/Thunder

Says the muse: I shall give you hunger, and pain, and sleepless nights.
Also beauty, and satisfactions known to few, and glimpses of the heavenly life.
None of these you shall have continually,
and of their coming and going you shall not be foretold.

—Howard Lindsey

Taoist Master Al Chung-Liang Huang explains that Hexagram 42 is symbolized by a wooden boat moving forward, driven by the wind. When wind and thunder, signifying action, cooperate, their power is doubled. The tide is turning in your favor and opportunities are coming your way. Pour it on now—if you're working on a manuscript, increase your work time and word count. If you have been contemplating a plan, jump in. Make tough decisions, tackle difficult projects, and forge ahead.

It is likely that during this period you will be called on to help others so that they too can succeed. If you are called on to lead, do so with confidence. Respond with generosity and relationships will benefit.

This is also the perfect time for self-improvement and attitude adjustment. During this favorable cycle, bad habits, attitudes, and self-indulgence can be discarded to make way for this new flow of energy.

Fiction Question:

Epiphany refers to a moment of truth when a character realizes something about himself or his world that he hadn't realized earlier. It generally overtakes the character with sudden brilliance and provides an insight that changes him.

Sometimes this self-truth can be sparked by an extraordinary event, but the epiphany often occurs in quiet or ordinary moments. Aristotle believed the epiphany was the power source of fiction. It can be the story's most dramatic moment or it can be portrayed more subtlety. Often, stories are structured around a series of epiphanies, and these realizations create the core of the character's transformation.

Epiphanies can be implanted in short stories and occur in classic works such as *The Metamorphosis*, *A Portrait of the Artist As a Young Man*, *Heart of Darkness*, and *The Island of Dr. Moreau*.

Depict an epiphany in its four parts: a setup that prepares the character for the understanding; a trigger, usually from an incident or outer source; the actual realization; and the proof that the epiphany has changed the character. For example, *A Christmas Carol* is constructed around a series of epiphanies, and by the story's end Scrooge is changed by these understandings.

Nonfiction Question:

The first advice that writers hear is to "write what you know." While crafting nonfiction, this is a well-meant adage, but perhaps better advice is to write about subjects that just won't leave you alone.

Most of us cannot afford to travel to Siberia for material and don't hobnob with the rich and famous. But you know what it feels like to grow up in a small Minnesota town, or Queens, or rural Alabama. And you know that your childhood memories are like restless ghosts whispering your name. You can write about the worries that find you sleepless in the middle of the night and the regrets that haunt you. You can write about the person you wish you had married, the children you never bore, or the child you gave up for adoption. If your heroes have always been baseball players and you've spent every summer of your life playing the game and following a team, write about the boy in the man and the heft of the bat. You can write about what your body has taught you, and how you see your role in the world.

Your passions and hauntings define you. From these secret and whispering places, write with authenticity and passion that will inspire readers.

The Writer's Path:

Confidence underlies all success. But while this statement might sound obvious, confidence is a complicated attribute in a writer's life. You build confidence through a series of successes, day by day.

Confidence also comes from research, preparation, and experimenting. It results from small gains—meeting a deadline, finding the perfect metaphor, and polishing a paragraph until it gleams.

Confidence comes from carefully listening to your critics, then making decisions about the validity of their feedback.

Confidence comes from attending writing conferences and book signings where the energy, optimism, and tools you acquire act like a vitamin boost.

Confidence comes from recalling all your successes in all parts of your life, then applying these skills and attributes to writing.

---

43. Deciding: Lake/Heaven

Poke around.

—William Carlos Williams

Even though it might not feel like it, the energy of the universe is on your side. An ancient interpretation of this hexagram suggests that it's a bad idea to approach an enemy or government office carrying arms. Another image depicts dredging a channel so that a river cannot overflow, signifying resolution and eliminating hesitation.

It is likely that you need to make a decision or are struggling with a problem. No matter what it pertains to, a visible stance is called for and compromise is not possible. This issue is not going to disappear of its own accord, so face the situation squarely. You must also bring secrets into the light and face facts. Once the truth is out in the open, your response must be reasonable, measured, and firm. Proceed carefully, while at the same time never backing down.

It's not easy, but it is possible to work for change without damaging other people or their reputations. If another person is the obstacle, treat him or her with respect and diplomacy. If you are having trouble with a child, focus on his or her better qualities. Constructive criticism, not blame, will work best now. It's also a good time to bury the past and look toward a healthier future in a relationship.

As in many situations, first you must determine that you are not the problem. Once you make that determination, don't focus on your weaknesses, but rather on solutions to overcome your flaws.

Fiction Question:

Desire drives plot. Know what your protagonist wants, and wants badly, and your story can be shaped around this knowledge. In every scene your protagonist wants something, and in every story he desperately wants it: to fall in love, to win the race, to solve the crime, to avenge his sister's rape, to find the truth, to find his birth mother, to obtain a bone marrow transplant. If a protagonist reacts only to external factors in the plot, it will fall short. Desire lends meaning to a story but it also propels it. Every act, choice, and decision is linked to your protagonist's desire.

An easy method for understanding your protagonist is to write this sentence: The thing my protagonist wants more than anything in the world is_____ .

The protagonist also sometimes acts to avoid something. He resists falling in love because last time, it ended in disaster. What your character fears is often the flip side of desire, and the two are often entwined in many plots. A protagonist may be forced to confront what he fears most, and once this fear is overcome, he wins his desire.

The elements that will thwart your character's desire will make the plot sizzle. Character flaws and emotional baggage will serve to block desire and define the protagonist. Desire must also be accurately linked to your protagonist's background. An atheist will not desire an audience with the Pope, just as a hopeless romantic won't want to settle for a platonic relationship.

Nonfiction Question:

Secrets and demons have a powerful draw in nonfiction. Readers want to travel into forbidden or formerly hidden places. And every writer has them. Perhaps you harbor secrets about a parent's alcoholism, your brother's suicide, or your partner's sex fetish. Perhaps you've battled drug addiction, compulsions, or depression. Perhaps suicide or mental illness is your family legacy.

These topics require more than simple revelation. They require an intimate viewpoint, the writer reaching some profound truth about the subject and allowing the reader into these dark and moving experiences.

As an exercise, collect essays and memoirs where writers divulge their secrets and demons. Note how far they go in tracing the truth, when they hold back, and when you were shocked or disappointed. Do the secrets seem tame, or written for shock value?

The more intimate and difficult the topics you write about, the more helpful it can be to analyze how other writers manage this same emotional territory.

The Writer's Path:

Wishful thinking is a childish approach to life. You wish that things would be better, that there was more time for your writing. You wish that you wrote like Hemingway or Capote or Anita Shreve. Or you sigh about how other writers have experienced big breaks or undeserved luck. But luck is made, not longed for. And wishes are nothing without action. Only action coupled with determination solves the problems inherent in the writing path.

If you have chosen this hexagram, it is likely that a problem has been brewing for a while, a bad habit has been festering, or a relationship has been deteriorating. It can no longer be ignored or wished away. Create a realistic battle plan. Face it like a grownup with resolve, a will of steel, and unbending optimism.

44. Making Contact: Heaven/Wind

The act of writing is an act of optimism. You would not take the trouble to do it if you felt it didn't matter.

—Edward Albee

The earliest image of this hexagram portrays a married couple; in later centuries the image stood for lovemaking. But like all symbology in the *I Ching,* the meanings of this hexagram are complex. With the wind blowing under heaven, it encounters everyone. Sometimes unworthy people are met, and sometimes temptations cross your path.

Trust your instincts, especially when dealing with people. There is an old saying that opposites attract, but in real life, when dealing with opposites, the situation is ripe for trouble. Find people and projects that suit you best. Don't fall for flattery or be fooled by those without integrity. And don't expect too much from new acquaintances.

If there is a deal on the table, read the fine print. There are possible dangers, especially if a situation seems innocent or looks too good to be true. Speak your mind; make certain that others know that you're not a pushover.

Hexagram 44 also warns of giving in to temptation and clinging to a bad habit that you have outgrown. These habits can take many forms, such as being wishy-washy, gullible, or lacking in business savvy. Negative thinking must also be addressed.

Fiction Question:

One of the clearest depictions of the sizzle of opposites occurs in the film *The African Queen*. In Africa during the First World War, a hard-drinking riverboat owner lets a straitlaced missionary persuade him to use his boat to attack a German warship. Charlie Allnut, a cigar-smoking, unshaven drifter and captain of the temperamental tramp steamer *The African Queen*, is played by Humphrey Bogart. Rose Sayer, played by Katharine Hepburn, is devoted to her brother's mission and is prissy, imperious, and tough.

It is a film about love conquering all as we watch Charlie, a broken man, discover hope and happiness in loving Rose. Rose also finds love and meaning from Charlie. While the story goal for their journey down the Ulonga-Bora is to destroy the German ship, the real prize lies in overcoming the psychological and emotional obstacles that stand between them.

When two opposites are on the stage, or on the page in fiction, the sizzle is palpable. But it doesn't necessarily need to occur in romance. In the movie *Freaky Friday* a mother and her teenage daughter change bodies and discover their shared humanity. Opposites naturally create conflict. In writing about opposites, consider this tip from author Barnaby Conrad: "If you want to know your characters better, ask yourself: How would they behave in a quarrel?"

Nonfiction Question:

Stories about temptation are as old as Adam and Eve, and temptation in all its forms is another topic with fascinating potential. You are tempted on a daily basis to yield to something that is not good for you. Temptation often has to do with giving in to short-term payoffs rather than waiting for long-term rewards. And this tug of war between rational thoughts and emotional desires can be fascinating. Think about temptation in all its beguiling forms: the adulterous affair, the jewelry, vacation, or car you cannot afford but splurge on anyway. The times you should be working, but instead are on the couch watching HBO.

Or consider small temptations, such as arriving at your office firm in your commitment to lose ten pounds only to discover that your desk mate has brought in three dozen Krispy Kreme doughnuts—your downfall. You can smell them, and no matter how you work to push their sugary taste out of your thoughts, you're dizzy with desire.

Temptation is everywhere, since our economy relies on tempting consumers with goods—often things we cannot afford. Car companies create gleaming new models each year aimed at luring consumers to trade up. And high-tech devices are constantly being upgraded and made slicker. It all adds up to temptation. Does yielding to it mean that you're weak—or merely human?

The Writer's Path:

Just as families can be dysfunctional, so can writers' groups. Sometimes you can easily spot whether a group is off track or is a negative influence on your writing. But sometimes you can waste valuable energy or be wrongly influenced by a dysfunctional writing group.

There are a few red flags to pay attention to, such as if an individual or the group as a whole is not motivated. Writers need to be hungry for success, determined to accomplish goals and get the writing done. If group members regularly show up without their "assignments," it's usually a signal that you're in the wrong group.

Notice too if any members are hostile, tactless, or seem to harbor a personal agenda. Some writers see themselves as saviors and are determined to transform everyone's writing to meet their standards.

Writing groups that are unfocused and undisciplined are also dysfunctional. Members spend too much time quaffing wine, complaining about how they don't have time to write, or chatting about their children. A healthy group assembles and immediately sets to work at the job at hand: improving each other's writing.

45. Gathering Together: Lake/Earth

You can never know enough about your characters.

—W. Somerset Maugham

In the original symbol for Gathering Together, thick bundles of grass represent assembling or collecting things. With lake over earth, the ancient Chinese believed that the nurturing waters of the lake represented an important gathering place. Combined with the stable forces of the earth, it means unity, good fortune, and prosperity.

Pay attention to the power of the group and the importance of relationships and true leadership. Although the possibilities for a good outcome are strong, it won't happen without effort. Another image associated with this hexagram is of a king making an offering at his ancestral temple. The king represents a wise leader, so make sure that the group's efforts and your own plans are carried out with logic and foresight. Assess your role, anticipate what might go wrong, and take steps to circumvent it.

Think about how unity works in large and small ways, how it applies to situations and writing. Gain strength and ideas from groups of writers and great writers who inspire you. Be responsive, alert, and balanced.

Fiction Question:

As you craft your novel, apply this checklist for elements that belong in fiction with a special emphasis on assessing your cast:

- Create a protagonist who is changed profoundly by events of the story.
- Involve your protagonist and other cast members in a situation where they are in over their heads.
- Create a "cauldron" or an untenable situation that the cast cannot escape from while the drama heats up.
- Shape characters who always act in ways that drive the story forward.
- Invent characters with deep motivations, convictions, and beliefs.
- Create a set of dominant personality traits for your main characters so that the reader has a clear understanding of them from the first time they appear on the page.
- Force your protagonist into new physical and emotional landscapes as the story progresses.
- Create a cast for several reasons, but also to reveal many sides of your protagonist. These extras include pets, siblings, friends, a sidekick, grandparents, and co-workers.
- Understand that a character's name elicits powerful first impressions. Use generation-appropriate names, as well as those that reflect a region, class, or culture.
- Don't mistake personality for character—character is the inner

world of your story people.

• Make certain that your characters don't sound alike when
they talk.

Nonfiction Question:

Once you are inspired by a topic, your next step is to choose the focus and structure so that you can say what needs to be said. Before you begin, brainstorm the possibilities for your piece.

Clustering, a brainstorming process described in Gabriele Rico's *Writing the Natural Way*, is a helpful technique to gather ideas within a short time. Clustering awakens the power of the right brain, which is associative and your source of inspiration. Clustering also helps focus on a single idea and breaks through resistance to writing.

On a blank page, write the nucleus word or phrase in the center and then circle it. Now, quickly jot down all the images and words that come to mind when you think about it. Write these words or phrases, each in its own circle, radiating from the center like the spokes of a wheel. Connect each new association with a line attaching it to the nucleus or the circled word that came before it. When a new connection strikes you, return to the nucleus and begin drawing circles and lines from the center again. Hint: When you're seeking associations to the nucleus, link your memory to your senses, such as trying to recall smells.

The Writer's Path:

At some point, most writers need a mentor. A mentor serves best when he or she is directly involved in your life, as in a teacher-student relationship. The best mentors point the way, lend you courage, and inspire with their greatness. If you don't have a mentor, find one. If you live in a small town or rural area, find inspiration by following an accomplished author's career from afar.

If you're fortunate enough to spend time with a mentor one on one, be respectful of his time. Don't waste time complaining about how it's impossible to break into Hollywood. Ask him probing questions that no one else can answer. Ask him how he made his way in his career and about his mistakes and how he corrected them. And if possible, repay his generosity with gratitude and by trying harder.

A caveat here: Don't seek out a mentor until you've paid your dues as a writer. A mentor can never take the place of hard work and can never act as a shortcut to learning the craft.

And here is another idea. If you find a mentor, spend time analyzing what this person has taught you. Find a photo of your mentor and paste it into the middle of a blank page. Then fill the page with all the wisdom this person has taught you. And when it is your turn to help a young writer along, pass it on.

---

46. Aim High: Earth/Wind

A poem is a way of life.

—Eloise Klein Healey

The stable earth over the yang energy of wind below signifies quick and powerful momentum. Like a kite in the wind, you can soar. This hexagram relates to advancement in many areas of life and shines a bright spotlight on success. You might feel that you're finally succeeding after a period of laying the groundwork. You've made steady progress and developed your skills.

Dare to dream—in fact, dream big. Since you've laid the foundation, go meet your success. Just keep your wits about you, keep working, and don't settle for less than you deserve. Your successes should enhance rather than threaten relationships.

Aim High also bodes well for a helpful person to assist with your next step. Take advantage of these opportunities and approach authority figures with confidence. Promote yourself and expect positive outcomes. Pursue social contacts and anticipate breakthroughs in communication with friends or relatives.

Fiction Question:

Crafting fiction requires understanding the foundational aspects of it. Use this list to determine if your understanding is on track.

- Create an inciting incident that rocks the protagonist's world, sets the plot in motion, and creates the first goal.
- Always draft a plot that stems from adversity.
- Make certain that all your major characters have an agenda.
- Foreshadow the most important scenes, especially the climax.
- Make certain that the protagonist, however reluctantly, takes charge of events.
- Determine that nothing should happen at random, and that most actions cause other actions.
- Devise a setting that creates a vivid and intricate world.
- Shape a plot based on a single dramatic question or conflict.
- Make certain that each chapter and most scenes ratchet up the tension.
- Let readers understand why villains do what they do.
- Write about the most important or interesting segment in your characters' lives.
- Choose the protagonist based on how he or she will be most changed by the story events.

Nonfiction Question:

Nonfiction writers need to understand the big picture, with a special understanding of what readers and editors are looking for in well-crafted essays and memoirs.

- Don't write for yourself; write for a reader, respecting his need to be informed, inspired, and entertained.
- Don't write to whine, vent, or obtain payback.
- Work hard at developing a distinctive voice—the memorable and authentic sound of you on the page.
- While some subjects require a light or humorous approach, work for the most part at exploring meaningful themes.
- Find ways to weave in data, straight-on facts, and knowledge so that the information doesn't bog down the whole.
- Use narrative techniques.
- The more emotional the subject, the more you should strive to use subtlety, not melodrama or sentimentality, in your approach.
- Write to evoke the reader's emotions.
- As in fiction, reflect conflict whenever possible.
- Write for the senses.
- Write from a questioning frame of mind and make certain that your attitude toward the subject is revealed.

The Writer's Path:

This hexagram advises you to aim high, but dreams without a solid plan in place are meaningless. It's time now to construct a five-year plan as if you were the CEO of your own corporation. Writers, like most professionals—contractors, marketers, political operatives, and retailers—must proceed with a blueprint for success. Too many writers wrongly assume that by sitting at a desk and typing away, they're creating a career. But all they're actually doing is typing. Many languish because their writing doesn't improve or never meets the standards of the industry. They haven't created a plan for improvement or getting published.

A five-year plan is practical and empowering. Select your most important goals, and then break them down into assignments that contain methods to build your skills. Include specific goals, such as spending three hours every morning at your desk or joining a class. Once your plan is in place, remember that creating a career is an ongoing process. Then, every six months or so, revisit your plan and make adjustments.

47. Restriction: Lake/Water

There are three rules for writing a novel.
Unfortunately, no one knows what they are.

—W. Somerset Maugham

With the lake over water, this means that the lake is empty. With double yin properties in Hexagram 47, the situation is confining, even imprisoning. If you find yourself feeling exhausted, trapped, or anxious, keep the faith. The restrictions that surround you do not exist merely to cause suffering. Restriction can bring benefits, even if at first you cannot recognize them. While the situation might appear oppressive, it will not last. It is vital that you believe in yourself now, so remain stable, optimistic, and calm.

You are being called on to gather your strength and bide your time. You are also required to have integrity even if you feel oppressed or threatened. Don't waste energy; wait out the storm with resolve and faith. Don't attempt to convince other people—your words will have little effect. Be absolutely unshaken in your beliefs, strength, and convictions. Be cautious of following blindly, especially if another person appears rash. You are most revealed when the going gets tough. Prove that you can handle adversity with grace and will.

Fiction Question:

Fictional characters are tested by adversity, which serves many purposes in a story. It provides the conflict that pushes the story forward; it proves that the protagonist is capable of change; it shows that he is worthy of achieving goals; it portrays him as vulnerable and flawed; it reveals the protagonist when he acts, decides, and chooses.

When creating adversity, use both inner and outer conflict. Physical adversity runs the gamut: pain, injury, death, illness, and discomfort. Adversity also includes lies, secrets, and all kinds of miscommunication such as crossed signals, misreading people, or misunderstanding another character.

Your character's inner conflict can take on many forms, with him worrying, yearning, weighing things, and making difficult, if not impossible, choices. For example, in your suspense novel your detective might be struggling to crack a big case and working impossible hours, but meanwhile, his elderly mother's health is failing. He needs to solve the crime because the criminal is a danger to society, but if his mother dies, he'll never have a chance to be with her again. Inner conflict often involves guilt and is often linked to the character's past. If your detective and his mother were extremely close, or if they had been estranged and had finally mended the relationship, his dilemma is especially difficult.

Another form of adversity is displacement, the fish-out-of-water or stranger-in-a-strange-land sort, which can be as simple as sending a shy person to a party or a novice on a mission that is beyond his skill level. Another tip to keep in mind when writing fiction, is that most relationships bring about suffering.

Nonfiction Question:

Life is often not fair. Most of us learn this harsh truth in childhood, a realization that can be scarring or enlightening. Unfairness comes in many shapes and sizes. Some children are picked on by a bully, watch as a sibling receives more favor or attention, or are born into families where they just don't fit in. In adulthood unfairness still carries the same sting: a boss who is unreasonable or abusive, bad luck or bad health, financial disasters, and the loss of loved ones. Our hearts get broken, people let us down, or a drunk driver careens into an innocent.

Apparently, whoever wrote the rules of life didn't include fairness on the list. Luckily, the human spirit, and more specifically the writer's spirit, can not only endure but survive pains large and small. Since misery often provides fruitful subjects, write about unfairness, but think deeply about what a reader can learn through your revelations.

Kvetching about misery is easy; transforming pain is the real medicine you're after. So take that extra step: Create a thoughtful analysis that portrays the human spirit and expresses your vulnerability. Find the gifts that you gained from unfairness, the ones that were so hard won. Perhaps hardship made you resilient or determined. Perhaps it taught you compassion for those who are less fortunate.

The Writer's Path:

In *The War of Art: Break Through the Blocks and Win Your Inner Creative Battles*, Steven Pressfield defines resistance, claiming it is invisible, internal, and insidious. He writes: "Resistance cannot be seen, touched, heard, or smelled. But it can be felt. We experience it as an energy field radiating from a work-in-potential. It's a repelling force. It's negative. Its aim is to shove us away, distract us, and prevent us from doing our work."

Resistance sometimes feels suffocating, or is disguised as indifference or grandiose fantasies. Other guises include doubt, obsessive thoughts, or worrying. Sometimes you experience it as distractions: you organize pens, books, and paperclips, balance your checkbook, and obsessively check email. Instead of writing. Resistance is often outfitted with rationalizations, excuses, and procrastination. Sometimes it shows up as numbness or apathy. Sometimes it is so sneaky that you are not even aware that it's ruining your creative output, much less your life.

So how do you fight resistance? First, understand that resistance is not writer's block, so call it by its proper name. Next, outwit it by acknowledging it and writing through it. Understand that there will be days when you write a lot, days when you write a few worthy sentences, and days when you're mostly incubating ideas. Create solid strategies and routines to follow day after day, and eventually resistance, while not always conquered, will be tamed.

---

48. The Depths: Water/Wind

A word is a bud attempting to become a twig. How can one not dream while writing? It is the pen which dreams. The blank page gives the right to dream.

—Gaston Bachelard

Hexagram 48 is sometimes referred to as The Well or The Source because it speaks of a deep source of nourishment and meaning that supports and connects us all. The images for The Depths are of a well, but also of watering parched ground. The Depths contain an inexhaustible source for replenishing.

This hexagram applies to your life in several ways. While water is a gift from the earth, it, like other resources, should never be wasted. Look deeply for answers; they will not be found in shallow places or among shallow people. Go within for guidance and self-development. The symbol of a well also reminds you to look beneath the surface of things, following your instincts and responding accordingly. Using your intuition about relationships is especially recommended.

If you are part of an organization, make certain that the values of the group are not superficial or inhumane. If you are called to lead a group, do so with integrity, working toward the common good. Communicate freely and honestly and you'll inspire others.

This is another hexagram that nudges you to serve others, so extend yourself and you'll be rewarded. Also use your inner guidance to solve problems rather than waiting for help.

Fiction Question:

While plotting requires creating a road map, there are also times when you need to allow the story its organic evolution. Fiction characters can take on a life of their own, start whispering commands, or voicing dialogue that you hadn't planned in the scene. Sometimes a secondary character becomes more important to the story than you first imagined. Or as you write, you discover deeper meanings or themes. Perhaps you'll realize that a subplot is needed to add more complications.

No matter what your outline dictates, if these changes deepen the story rather than muddy it, go with them. Yes, planning makes a writer's job easier, but it should not be the jail that you write from. And if you preplan every aspect of the story, you'll miss the great joy of writing fiction, which is responding to the story that unfolds and allows your characters to speak to you.

Nonfiction Question:

Spirituality is not only a cohesive force in your life, but also a source of writing. Whatever their spiritual beliefs, all writers tap into some source to find inspiration. And for those writing about spirituality and beliefs, it is an opportunity to get published while exploring life's mysterious forces.

Luckily, there are a number of writing experts who have written about the topic. Julia Cameron, Natalie Goldberg, and Anne Lamott all make a living at writing about how their creativity and writing skills intersect with their spirituality. Each has her own set of beliefs and each claims these beliefs and practices as the source for writing. If you've chosen this hexagram it is also time to deepen your spiritual connections.

The Writer's Path:

No matter your age or your circumstances, you have access to a limitless source of ideas and creativity. This source holds glories and inspiration, a constant, simmering bounty. If you have selected this hexagram, you need to be reminded of this. If your creativity is wavering, return to your source, whatever it may be. Find what stirs you, but also realize that you are not alone. Your creative source is within and all around you.

As you tune in to your source, notice the form it takes in your life. Some writers find inspiration from the small voice within. Some writers are inspired by children. Others find inspiration in nature, in church, or during meditation or prayer. The source is always with you, in your lonely hours and when your doubts are nagging. Tap the energy of your source. Make your inner life and connecting to this source your primary concerns now. Creativity is always miraculous and generous, an infinite, powerful partner.

49. Transformation: Lake/Fire

*To publish one story, encouraging and pleasant as that may be,
is not the key. The key is to find the place in you where the stories you can
write—want to write, even need to write—are. The thing is not merely to get
there and bring back a single story, not to find a single piece of glowing
amber but then learn to recognize the glow, to study the route to the place of
the stories, so that you can find your way back there again, even if the walls
of the tunnel have caved in behind you on your way out.*

—Thomas E. Kennedy

Imagine a cocoon transforming into a butterfly or a snake shedding its skin. The power of renewal and transformation is intense now. Transformation is not a violent overthrow of what has been, but rather a focused recreating.

Joseph Campbell described the *I Ching* as "a kind of geometry of mythology.... It tells of the readiness of time and the art of moving with its tides, rocking with the waves." It is now time to rock with the waves that surround you.

Try a new approach; even consider drastic changes. If a manuscript is faltering, mull over a complete overhaul. But radical changes are never undertaken without appropriate planning and study. Don't discard the old simply because you're restless or dissatisfied. New, careful approaches, not quick fixes, are called for along with the shedding of outmoded efforts. Think in terms of gradual, step-by-step changes. After all, the butterfly does not emerge with its bright wings overnight. As in nature, the timing for your change is essential.

Fiction Question:

Character arc is the term given to a series of changes whereby a character journeys from one way of being at the beginning of a story to another at the end. Often this is a journey of understanding or belief. He can change from a mean drunk to a person of compassionate sobriety, from cheating to honesty, from someone who has given up on life to someone renewed by hope.

Some stories call for a character to change from good to bad, but most often a character changes from bad to good or weak to strong. Ebenezer Scrooge is an example of a character undergoing a dramatic character arc. However, the more drastic the change, the more the writer needs to provide proof of the transformation via new acts and decisions and the motivations that caused them.

Character arc begins on page one, or in the opening scene of a film, as when Kathleen Turner plays the isolated, timid workaholic writer in the film *Romancing the Stone*. By the final scenes she is not only brave and adventurous, but has turned into the sort of femme fatale that she writes about. Character arc can also be a means to heal an emotional wound, as when FBI Agent Clarice Starling in *The Silence of the Lambs* faces the loss of her father.

Character arc is compelling for many reasons. It creates conflict because the protagonist will resist change, and if he doesn't change something horrible will happen. Generally the climax showcases the protagonist drawing on his new strengths and hard-won lessons in order to survive. Thus, the climactic scenes are where the arc is completed and his new persona is revealed.

Nonfiction Question:

There is nothing quite as satisfying as reading a novel in which a character undergoes a vital and dramatic transformation. But nonfiction can also be shaped around transformation. Think about it. Giving birth to their firstborn dramatically transforms a couple's existence. A cancer diagnosis or heart attack brings about transformation, as do falling in love, falling out of love, or having a bold stroke of luck.

Readers have an intrinsic fascination with watching other people undergo change. Write about transformation including all its joys and struggles.

The Writer's Path:

In long-ago China one message of this hexagram was that silt in the bottom of a well needed to be removed. Silt muddies or contaminates water, but removing the silt isn't easy. Various other meanings of this hexagram speak about abolishing the old to make way for something new and better.

The realization that a manuscript is not working and likely needs a major overhaul is one of the most difficult aspects of writing. In fact, it's one of the worst parts of the writing path. If you have chosen this hexagram, take heart. Many successful authors have created a publishable story from the ashes of an old draft.

Courage, steadiness, and clarity are called for now. Your approach must encompass analyzing the major aspects such as structure, characterization, pacing, and purpose.

---

50. The Cauldron: Fire/Wind

Learning to write is learning who you are.

—Marshall Cook

The symbol from antiquity in this hexagram is of a sacred vessel, perhaps owned by a dynasty and used in offerings and ceremonies. The Cauldron refers to the individual existing in and harmonizing with the cosmic order. If you are working toward the good of all, you will succeed and flourish. The Cauldron is a powerful omen, especially for artists, as it speaks of potential and possibilities.

Search for meaning in your work and life and avoid selfish pursuits. Your ideas are sound, but your skills might need polishing and perfecting.

Don't chase easy money or status. Instead, base goals on spiritual values. Readjust and realign yourself so that you are in harmony with the larger world. Both business and personal relationships can be transformed, renewed, or developed. You can be an inspiring presence, a true friend.

The Cauldron reminds you that there are times when it is wise to accept your fate, and this is one of them. You needn't be a passive follower; rather, realize that sometimes an invisible and mysterious force is at work. Surrender and accept your present circumstances. You will be empowered and renewed when fate is on your side.

Fiction Question:

In fiction you construct a situation that forces characters to come together and stick together. This is commonly called the cauldron or crucible. In the cauldron, the characters are trapped together and the drama, enflamed by conflict, simmers, boils, and spills over.

Many writers devise their cauldron unconsciously—it simply arrives with the story idea. But once you've chosen your cauldron, make certain that the characters are forced to interact because of its constraints. The cauldron represents a microcosm. Typical cauldrons can be a family, a workplace, a board of directors, a group project, a neighborhood, or an apartment building.

Famously, *The African Queen* thrusts two unlikely characters together on a boat on an African river, and their common cause and humanity transform both. Or in Michael Crichton's *Disclosure*, characters struggle in the cutthroat Seattle computer industry. When you formulate your cauldron, remember that there can be no easy escape.

Nonfiction Question:

The Cauldron presents an intriguing suggestion for nonfiction writers. Consider developing a memorable brand—similar to a trademark— and a style that resonates with it. Branding is the identifying image that people associate with a company, product, web site, or individual. It creates loyalty, trust, recognition, and for writers, a platform.

The most successful authors of our age find a niche and then brand themselves as experts in it. Deepak Chopra, Suze Orman, and Dr. Phil McGraw are current examples.

But not all topics need to be written strictly for consumers. Julia Cameron writes about creativity, Noam Chomsky writes about politics, and Jon Krakauer, author of *Into Thin Air* and other books, writes about adventure.

Branding is linked to your master plan, imagining your goals for the next five, ten, or twenty years.

The Writing Path

There are so many aspects of the writing life to keep in mind as we work on our novels, memoirs or poems, but here's a simple bit of advice: write, don't type. You see, often writers are merely typing when they are working on a project, putting down word after word without an adequate consideration of each word's effect on the reader and its contribution to the whole. Or, they write without an adequate understanding of the genre they're working in or an understanding of the underlying structure of a screenplay, novel, or essay. The advice here is to slow down and analyze your skill level, then once you spot your weaknesses, correct them and move up to the next level.

Build your skills by reading books about craft and analyzing published works. Start a word list, collecting a vocabulary of solid, specific nouns and vivid verbs. Find words that contain onomatopoeia and add them to your arsenal. Carry a writer's notebook whereby you hone your awareness of the everyday world by jotting down interesting conversations, notes about books you're reading, description of fascinating strangers, or remembrances of a fabulous dinner party. Collect, notice, and write with thought and planning.

---

51. Shake Up: Thunder/Thunder

The essence of drama is that man cannot walk away
from the consequences of his own deeds.

—Harold Hayes

Imagine a thunderstorm that shakes the earth and sky with its force. Nature is mighty and sometimes frightening. Unexpected events can also shock or scare us. If something unseen has happened, don't panic. Remind yourself that although the situation is unsettling, the outcome will be positive. The mature person realizes that life is not predictable, and learns to cope with its ups and downs.

In the aftermath of a shakeup, keep your head and recognize the opportunity for a new direction. This shakeup might pertain to a burden or stagnation that you needed to have wrested from you. Surrender it gladly and embrace new possibilities.

Storms, once they pass, sweeten the earth. And shakeups, even though sometimes painful, cause growth and fresh insights. Dwell on the positive rather than the destructiveness of change. The outcome is a new cycle that is easier, and more relaxed, creative, and enjoyable.

Fiction Question:

Fictional plots zigzag so that tension percolates throughout; twists, surprises, and setbacks often occur when the reader least expects them. Reversals, meaning that a character experiences a reversal of fortune or events turn upside down, are used in most plot structures. For example, in a mystery novel the detective is closing in on a suspect, but then the suspect is murdered too, so he must change direction and search for the real killer. In a romance, the couple is finally drawing close when a misunderstanding throws a wrench into matters, creating distrust. These new events are not easily resolved, and prevent the story from becoming predictable.

A major reversal occurs at the midpoint: the hunter becomes the hunted, the protagonist discovers he can't trust someone he's trusted before, he wins something he was sure he'd lost, or an adversary turns out to be an ally. Whatever the mid point reversal, your protagonist is faced with drastically changed circumstances and must scramble to adapt. All reversals force your protagonist to dig within himself to find new resources, and the results make him change his beliefs and assumptions.

Reversals begin with the inciting incident, when your protagonist's world is disrupted, then continue like dominoes toppling. Remember that drama works well when things are *not* going as the character expected or hoped.

Nonfiction Question:

Nonfiction requires a range of speeds and rhythms along with twists and turns to keep the reader engaged. Consider the speed of things and how you sometimes want a reader to pause, while at other times you want to raise his pulse.

A simple method of playing with pacing is to vary your sentence length. Long sentences have a forward rolling motion that carries the reader along. Medium-length sentences are fine for delivering information. Short sentences force him to slam on the brakes. Single-word sentences are the ultimate wake-up call. Pacing requires deliberate choices. Too many short sentences, and the work is choppy and the reader is annoyed. Too many long sentences or run-on sentences, and your reader gets lost.

Slow down for significance and when presenting complicated information that needs to be broken down. Slow down to create suspense and to focus on a moment of truth or significance.

The Writer's Path:

Envy is one the most poisonous emotions that can doom a writer. It is the cousin of self-pity and its dark tendrils can choke your heart, making you feel depressed, ashamed, and alone.

Envy can crop up when a rejection letter arrives, when a friend is published, when anyone's success seems to diminish your own. Perhaps a writer who is your daughter's age has made it to the big time while you're still struggling to gain a footing in the publishing world, or someone with lesser skills writes a breakout novel that you know is inferior to your own. You sigh; you wonder at fickle and cruel fate; you castigate yourself for your wrinkles and vulnerable heart.

The truth in the publishing world is often tough to swallow. Writers with little talent are published every day. Shallow or narcissistic memoirs make millions, and writers with the personality of Hannibal Lector acquire legions of adoring fans.

Quit expecting fairness and instead commit yourself to your own work, to improving, always improving. And finally, meet other writers to humanize your competition and learn to root for their successes.

—

52. Staying Centered: Mountain/Mountain

To get published you have to do what every writer in history has done.
You have to sit for thousands of hours and hundreds of days in solitude.

You have to read and write on a daily basis.
You have to be utterly vulnerable on the page,
and utterly ruthless in revision.
To write something good you have to want it so bad
that nothing else matters.

—Chris Offutt

This hexagram stands for a mountain with its strength, constancy, and stillness. The mountain also represents boundaries and limits, since its mass must be circumvented in order to move ahead.

Likewise, it is a time to recognize and respect your limits. If you are anxious or worried, you need to calm yourself, because fretting is useless. A troubled mind blocks your intuition and consequently your next productive steps.

Hexagram 52 advises you to find your bearings and to deeply assess the situation from a position of stability and stillness. If you're required to make a stand or confront some difficulty, don't allow it to deteriorate into drama.

It is likely that a cycle is ending, so with its passing don't dwell on what has happened before. Staying Centered doesn't refer to a situation but the frame of mind that you operate from. Meditation or other methods that train and quiet the mind will be beneficial.

Fiction Question:

Scenes are the building blocks of fiction, and unfold in front of the reader, causing worry and involvement. Each scene occurs for a reason, and is built around a character's goal and the opposition to that goal. Scenes contain sharply defined characters, preferably the protagonist who is going up against some obstacle. Emotional reversal is usually built into a scene; that is, the character feels differently at the ending than he did at the beginning. And the scene ending somehow pushes the reader to keep reading because it contains a cliffhanger or forces some new development. Scenes enrich or reveal characters, provide information, move the plot forward, or cast light on past events.

Scenes are made up of action, description, and exposition. The proportions of these three elements will vary depending on the needs of the scene, but generally action, including dialogue, will be the main ingredient. Description is required to make it real and participatory. Each scene takes place in a distinct time and place with specific details, such as a fishing wharf with dense fog rolling in.

Scenes are rarely written without dialogue, and dialogue is often a power struggle. Dialogue and action are the means by which you reveal that something important is happening.

Work to create a sense of urgency in scenes so that your characters must take immediate action. The opposition in scenes is always threatening, always portends some kind of change. If possible, surprise the reader in a portion of your scenes, but make certain that the surprise is not contrived. If a character's failure occurs in the scene, place this failure at the end.

Nonfiction Question:

Fifty years ago, when a writer had a story to tell, he usually wrote fiction. But a shift in trends and interest has taken place, and memoir writing now is a common means to recall experiences. This sea change is perhaps influenced by the fact that we live in a culture that is complicated and shifting, and in this shifting environment people want to testify. We also live amid a media culture that is more and more revealing, with tabloid journalism and reality television programs.

Readers buy memoirs to explore a life that has been lived and to find answers to fundamental questions about what it means to be alive. They want to understand the writer's particular brand of humanity and, in reading, to find meaning and direction in their own lives.

Memoirs have a structure; they are not merely a list of facts, dates, or memories. Instead, some common thread is woven through, connecting and unifying themes and ideas. The best memoirs transform the raw data of a life and shape it into deeper meaning. Memoirs provide a writer with a means to re-frame a life and discover what has mattered. It is the self under a microscope, and this honest scrutiny is illuminating. Memoirs also deeply delve into a cast of characters involved in the memoirist's life, and in these interactions and through discoveries, wisdom and truth are delivered. Details and emotional significance lift the memoir above simple reporting. But most of all a memoir is honest.

Tobias Wolff advises:

> If you're writing something you're going to call a memoir, I think you owe it to your readers to be as honest as you can. And that includes sometimes putting things in a memoir that may not make you proud, but are an essential part of the story. Other-wise you end up with a book in which you're the one who always has the virtue while everyone else does everything wrong. You're the one who always says the smart things while everybody else says the dumb things. That's just a way of going back and doing right what you didn't do right the first time. But it isn't very interesting.

The Writer's Path:

It's okay to emulate and admire other writers, but it is not okay to com-pare yourself to them and compete with them. There is nothing more deadly than the comparison game. The bigger the writer, the smaller you look.

Competing is lonely and demeaning. It wastes your creative energy. It feeds your insecurities and self-pity. You always lose.

There will always be writers like Stephen King and Joyce Carol Oates who are so prolific that it seems that they are channeling stories from the gods. Or writers like Alice Munro, whose prose contains such beauty and intricacy that you feel like an ugly duckling in comparison. If your literary heroes intimidate you, try reading their earliest works, or spend a month reading their whole body of work. In this way you'll see the progression of their techniques over time.

Notice how the best writers keep improving their craft, are constantly learning. Emulate strengths and you will become stronger. Remind yourself of the statement that Michelangelo made a week before his death: "I am still learning."

53. Patience: Wind/Mountain

Rewriting is like scrubbing the basement floor with a toothbrush.
—Pete Murphy

Hexagram 53 is named for the Jian River, which winds through vast stretches of central China. With its meandering path beginning in the mountains, it symbolizes gradual development and a breakthrough.

Although this is a good omen, no matter the situation, patience is called for. Keep moving forward even if progress seems slow. If you feel anxious to push ahead at full speed, restrain yourself. Have faith that matters will unfold exactly when they should and no sooner. One word to keep in mind is persistence.

Many *I Ching* hexagrams advise patience and calm, but in Hexagram 53, you are especially admonished to rein in emotions. In business matters, don't expect quick profits, promotions, or results. In relationships, spend time developing a deep, mutual understanding. Years ago in China this hexagram signified a long engagement as symbolized by the wild goose, which mates for life.

Avoid extreme lifestyles and curb your longing for freedom. Happiness might lie in more traditional ways of living. Once you understand what you truly want, you'll find traditions enriching rather than constraining. If you remain patient, optimistic, and centered, all will be well.

Fiction Question:

Writing a novel requires more patience than you may have thought possible. You'll discover that you're creating a puzzle of many pieces that don't seem to fit together as neatly as you imagined when you began. Sometimes when you're running low on patience, it's helpful to return to the blueprint for your story.

Here are the elements to keep you on track:

- Protagonist's name
- Protagonist's identity
- Protagonist's backstory
- Situation
- Story question
- Protagonist's goal
- Protagonist's motivation
- Plot journey
- Main obstacle/antagonist
- Internal conflict
- Time span
- Resolution

This blueprint will create your pitch, which is a succinct description of a story. Crafting a pitch is also helpful to keep you on track when writing your early drafts. A pitch is similar to the copy written on the back cover of a paperback or the jacket flap of a hardcover novel. Here is an example of one:

Desperate and out of work detective Al Huber must solve the murder of Michelle Barnard, his attractive next-door neighbor, if he is to survive a financial downturn and rebuild his shattered self esteem. But delving into Michelle's mysterious death unleashes doubts about his abilities, and death threats make him question if he'll survive the investigation and the criminal entanglements of the lovely Michelle.

Nonfiction Question:

Like a novel, a memoir requires a cast of characters, proving the veracity of your tale. Use real people to bring life and movement to your memoir, but also to set it apart from journalism, reports, and writing that isn't woven around a personal drama.

Characterization means the qualities, traits, and features that distinguish one person from another. Each person in your cast must be vivid, interesting, and differentiated. Notice the person's stance in the world, his or her typical movements, gestures, posture, speech, and keys to appearance. Bring real people to life by including at least one unusual physical characteristic such as hair color, unusual glasses, or mode of dressing.

A person who is central to your memoir will be described in greater detail than minor players. Don't write about types, use generalizations, or create an inventory. People become real when they talk. Listen for the individual speech patterns and expressions. Capture originality and flavors of speech, including regionalisms.

When writing about people, explore what they fear, believe, love, and hate. Use specific data, small scenes, or anecdotes that illustrate their importance in your life story.

Sometimes memoirists are required to bend the rules. For example, you might want to meld several people together to create a single person. Or, if you're writing about highly sensitive events such as abuse, you might want to disguise a villain. This doesn't suggest, however, that you invent people wholesale. Remember that your purpose is discretion, while telling the truth as you know it.

The Writer's Path:

When a writer crafts his first novel or lengthy project, small frustrations continually crop up. You scribble half a scene onto the page, but then are unsure where to end it. Sometimes you're able to write through the problem, but the results never quite satisfy you. At times, in order to save your sanity, you skip over trouble spots and move on to another chapter or character.

And then sometimes the writing swims along nicely only to sink again when another problem scene comes up. It is during these starts and stops that your patience wears thin, when you realize that you expected so much more from your abilities. You imagined that simply showing up at the page entitled you to have brilliant thoughts.

But you can discover after many drafts that patience in writing is the ability to cut yourself a little slack. There will be good days and less-than-productive days. When you encounter a story problem that doesn't budge, give it your best effort and then let it go. But letting it go doesn't mean you forget about it. Instead try this: Before an afternoon nap, or before turning in for the evening, set aside five minutes to meditate on the scene and the problems it contains. Look at the source of frustration from a distance, forgiving yourself for not being able to tackle it immediately.

Then remind yourself that you will be in the right place at the right time, writing the perfect paragraph or scene. Some writers will dream of solutions when they apply this method before sleep. Sue Grafton is known to write plotting problems onto slips of paper and tuck them under her pillow before sleeping. The solution often occurs only a day or so after she asks the question.

———

54. Subordinate Role: Thunder/Lake

Do what you can, with what you have, where you are.

—Theodore Roosevelt

In ancient times, this hexagram was called the Marrying Maiden and portrayed a young woman marrying a powerful man. Those familiar with Chinese society know she was often a concubine, and usually had little power or respect in her new household. Thus, although your current role might not grant you top billing, you need to accept it and work to make the best of things. Before agreeing to a subordinate role, you must weigh the advantages and disadvantages so that you can avoid resentment. Dignity is called for, and false pride and jealousy should be avoided.

It is possible that you will feel undervalued and overlooked now. Instead of struggling for justice, it's best to play along with the situation. After all, you know your true worth. If others don't recognize your value, nothing can be done about it for the time being. So don't waste energy trying to assert yourself, attempting to control other people, or blowing your horn. Carry on with grace, but at the same time don't allow yourself to be manipulated.

Like many aspects of life, this is a passing phase. Someday your greatness will be recognized and your writing will be appreciated. With pride in check, act agreeably and adapt to the situation. Also, with your long-range plans in mind at all times, you can endure and even thrive.

Fiction Question:

Secondary characters exist for many reasons: to entertain, to deepen the story, and to illuminate the protagonist and his world. They add freshness, color, and extreme behaviors and personalities. Writers also use them to introduce normalcy or ballast in the story.

Whatever the needs of your story, secondary characters are not mere props and cannot be thinly drawn. Include physical descriptions for important secondary characters and at least one memorable detail about each. Prove to readers that your minor characters are complex and rounded. Because the reader is not usually granted access to a secondary character's thoughts, they are understood through actions and dialogue.

While devising your cast, imagine their many uses. Employ secondary characters to provide contrasting emotions in dramatic moments. Use them to cause or orchestrate major events in the story, creating obstacles, surprises, and complications. Use secondary characters to enliven slow or too-quiet scenes or chapters. Remember that secondary characters can have their own goals, divided loyalties, crises, failures, and successes: in other words, reasons for living.

As when creating major characters, give secondary characters a dominant set of three or four personality traits—bravery, trustworthiness, honesty, sentimentality, hesitation, worry—that will be consistent in each scene, and provide a foundation of personhood.

Nonfiction Question:

While many subjects are covered in personal essays, it is often when we struggle to define our principles, values, and inner truths that our writing connects with the reader.

The writer makes the topic matter to the reader; it is not merely an abstract concept such as injustice or racism. It is nailed down by concrete details, specific examples, anecdotes, and metaphorical illustrations, and demonstrates where these concepts intersect with real life.

Your job as the writer is to convince your reader, paint the world that you're familiar with, describe inner truth as only you know it. The best essays show a thoughtful mind at work, pondering issues that you feel passionately about.

The Writer's Path:

When things are going well, it's easy to stay motivated. Editors answer your letters and grant assignments; your agent champions your latest manuscript. Staying motivated in bad times, through fatigue and rejection, is what separates a writer from an amateur.

Find creative ways to stay motivated, such as rewarding yourself with books or a night on the town after you achieve a certain goal. Take regular breaks to exercise and read widely to stay inspired. Invest in yourself by taking classes, buying books on technique, and attending conferences. As you work, realize that while writing is often a high, it can be daunting and difficult just as often.

And then take charge of your thinking. You need to expect peaks and valleys in your creativity and successes. You must also realize that drudgery is part of every profession, even those that look glamorous.

Finally, note Michele Weldon's advice:

> Erase the clutter of excuses about a lack of time, place or fear of how your words will look, and just write. Commit to the sanctity of your words with the same fervor and loyalty you would commit to a friend who needs you in a crisis or to an unavoidable work deadline demanded by a boss.

---

55. Harvest: Thunder/Fire

Good writers are those who keep the language efficient.

That is to say, keep it accurate, keep it clear.

—Ezra Pound

Favorable conditions exist, and you can fulfill your potential. This hexagram is like the full moon, the sun at midday, or the lush promise of early summer. You are at your peak, so take advantage of this phase—it will pass quickly. But instead of focusing on the inevitable waning, relish the now. Harvest what you've sown, and believe in yourself and your upcoming success. As you fulfill your potential, treat others with generosity.

Positive aspects can be found in dealing with the outside world, particularly the world of commerce and business. Resolve problems with tact and kindness. You should be able to see troubling situations with fresh clarity and objectivity.

Harvest suggests that it is the right time to send your work out to editors or agents. Trust that the future is beckoning and you can navigate whatever comes your way. Remain optimistic and confident in all you do and say. Try not to worry about the future; instead, nurture these feelings of strength so that you can carry them forward.

Fiction Question:

In your first draft, you are writing your heart out and writing quickly, as if on fire. Ray Bradbury says:

> I do a first draft as passionately and as quickly as I can. I be-lieve a story is valid only when it's immediate and passionate, when it dances out of your subconscious. If you interfere in any way, you destroy it… Let your characters have their way. Let your secret life be lived.

While writing your first draft you're staying close to that secret life, that early inspiration. That secret life is a magical place, and you cannot predict when a door opens into it. Author Robert Sheckley says:

Magic comes unexpectedly and always at the most inconvenient time; where you're falling asleep or getting on a plane or train. That's the moment to have a way already prepared to get words down—a notepad and pen, a cassette recorder, a laptop typewriter or computer.

Since this inspiration can fade, create conditions that invite the muse. Write at the same time every day, because this signals your subconscious that it's time for work. Try placing objects that remind you of your fictional world in your office, or play music that fuels your mood. Then simply write fast.

Keep your mind clear of judgments as you write your first draft. Don't try for stunts during this draft; write simply and quickly, imagining the protagonist's inner world. Let the story come forth from the regions of your imagination where it has been sleeping, waiting for this moment to awake you with its power. As the dream comes forth, write it down. Then write some more.

Nonfiction Question:

We all know sticky sentiment when we read it on the page. It's about adorable babies and puppies and kittens, and children clutching wilted dandelions. It's a mother's tears and a grandmother's lap and a fallen solider. It's about a child who is tragically ill, a lover who leaves without explanation, or an old man who can no longer hobble to his favorite fishing hole. All these topics can be made compelling or sickly, depending on the writer's choices and approach.

Sentiment is not easy to discern in your own writing, however. You are sometimes too close to the subject or cannot adequately judge your own work. But there is another issue: you must write stories that matter, about topics that make you feel deeply. By delving into them, you hope that your thoughts and emotions come through to the reader. And avoiding writing about such feelings means avoiding the risks inherent in writing. William Kittredge teaches that if you're not risking sentimentality, you are not writing close to your inner self.

But even as you feel deeply, remember that modern readers are turned off by sentimentality, so learn to discern sentiment from sentimentality. Emotions on the page must be heartfelt and true, while sentimentality is easy and gimmicky. Douglas Bauer, the author of *The Stuff of Fiction: Advice on Craft*, gives this suggestion:

> Sentiment is to sentimentality as artful eroticism is to artless pornography. In the first case, both the mind and the senses are aroused. Consequently, the impact is earned and it lingers intricately. But in the latter, only the senses are touched and the sensation disappears when the source is removed.

So think about it. Do your images linger intricately?

The Writer's Path:

Write because you need to write, because you tap into magic and find yourself during this process. Write because it makes you grow and proud of yourself. Do not become a writer because your husband, wife, mother, teacher, or best friend claims that you're a natural. Nor because your sister or aunt is a writer and it looks easy from a distance. Do not become a writer to fulfill your fantasies of a ten-city book tour and guest appearances on national television programs.

If you don't enjoy most parts of the writing process, chances are you won't accomplish much. And if you don't enjoy reading the genre you're writing in, you're also in the wrong business.

Write because you must. Write because it fills you up. Barbara Kingsolver offers this sound advice: "Close the door. Write with no one looking over your shoulder. Don't try to figure out what other people want to hear from you; figure out what you have to say. It's the one and only thing you have to offer."

---

56. Passing Through: Fire/Mountain

I believe in belief.

Sandra Flavin

Sometimes this hexagram is called Traveling because it suggests impermanence, which helps you see yourself as a traveler or sightseer. The situation, whether positive or trying, is temporary and change is in the air. Be ready to move on if necessary and don't cling to anything outmoded. As you pass through, avoid obvious traps and dead ends. Since you're in unfamiliar terrain (often without a map), chart a practical and realistic course. Don't trust strangers until they prove trustworthy.

This is not a time for overreaching or grandiose goals. It is a phase best suited to simple plans, self-reliance, short-term commitments, and gathering information. If a deal is underway, weigh your options carefully and make decisions that you can live with. If you're in unfamiliar territory, literally or figuratively, don't sell out in order to make friends or feel more comfortable.

Avoid long-term commitments in all things now. Proceed slowly, faithfully taking care of mundane matters and focusing on day-to-day duties. If you stay true to your ideals during this time, you will steer clear of problems. Just keep moving even if feels like you're plodding or that you are a stranger in a strange land. Although passing through might challenge your comfort zone, it's actually an opportunity for growth and self-discovery. What you'll discover is that your true security, and possibly even your identity, come from your own resources and integrity.

Fiction Question:

Many problems can befall a novel or story, but perhaps one of the deadliest is exposition that stops the story's progress. Exposition is the information necessary so that the reader can understand the fictional world and events. In historical fiction, science fiction, or fantasy, the reader requires explanations of how the world works because it's obviously not the world of the reader. But herein lies the trap: if a fantasy is a continuous explanation of a wizard's powers, historical feuds, and castle layout, the story will falter. After all, conflict must serve as the engine, and too much information causes the engine to sputter.

Yet in all sorts of fiction, facts, data, and background information clarify the culture, technology, geology, or mores. Facts and practical information are required for context. But this information cannot be delivered as a lecture and it cannot be included without a viewpoint. It might be helpful to think about Alfred Hitchcock's explanation for the success of his films. He said, "I leave out the boring parts of life."

So avoid history lessons and diatribes on how an engine works. When possible, put exposition within a character's viewpoint so readers watch or hear a character discover the world, making the facts more intimate. Or, if there is some form of technology, device, or plan in the story, demonstrate it failing so that the characters must fix it and the situation provides conflict.

Nonfiction Question:

Travel can inspire surprising insights. It is when you leave home that you can look at the world with new eyes and look back at your life from afar, seeing it with clarity. And travel provides many opportunities for writing. There is the thoughtful travel memoir, the essay that sparkles with perceptiveness, or the article that describes the indescribable. Editors need travelers to cover food trends, festivals, wine, accommodations, shopping, and historical aspects of travel. Because traveling is also beset with hazards like lost luggage and plane cancellations, it can also inspire humor or an advice piece.

So if you love beaches, islands, or cruise ships, these are places that can bring about stories. Cathedrals, art tours, and garden tours might also be your focus. Travel can produce a story on nearly any topic, but it all starts with seeing the place with an untarnished vision. And while you want to catch the wide shot of the place you're visiting, remember to home in on a few aspects of the trip. Editors want focused articles or remembrances, potent and loaded with details, so that the reader feels as if he is traveling with you. Reflect on what you found amazing, what you're certain you'll never encounter again. Then wrap it in word pictures and senses.

The Writer's Path:

May Sarton was a poet, novelist, and memoirist who produced luminous volumes. Her series of journals, particularly *Journal of a Solitude*, broke new ground and illustrated how a creative woman, living alone, had universal truths to tell. She could focus on afternoon light slanting in on a simple flower arrangement or hours spent gardening, and make you feel like you had entered her yard or parlor. And her life, spent among flowers, fellow writers, and books, was both quiet and rich with friendships, travel, and inspiration.

Her advice on writing and living holds simple truths as when she suggests this:

> I always forget how important the empty days are, how important it may be sometimes not to expect to produce anything, even a few lines in a journal. I am still pursued by a neurosis about work inherited from my father. A day where one has not pushed oneself to the limit seems a damaged, damaging day. Not so. The most valuable thing we can do for the psyche, occasionally, is to let it rest, wander, live in the changing light of a room.

57. Gentle Influences: Wind/Wind

What I like in a good author isn't what he says, but what he whispers.

—Logan Pearsall Smith

Sometimes life calls for boldness; at other times, subtlety. This is a time for following the wind and its gentle influences. Wherever you go, proceed with delicacy and acquiescence, and stay out of the limelight. If you're called on to be the influence behind the throne, accept the position with dignity and confidence. Keep an open mind, trusting that doors will open even if you're not banging on them in frustration. Be adaptable, and bend in the wind.

Another key to success during this period is to work steadily on your larger goals, never wavering from your lifetime purpose. Be clear in your intentions and keep your promises to yourself. Success is brewing now even if you cannot see it happening. Trust, believe in yourself, and stay focused.

This is another period in which it's best to keep your opinions to yourself. Patience in all things is called for, but especially if you're feeling overlooked or underutilized.

Fiction Question:

The power of suggestion in fiction cannot be exaggerated. Suggestive elements are used in dialogue, description, setting, and characterization—in fact, in every aspect of the story. One suggestive technique is subtext, which is emotions simmering beneath dialogue, illuminating what the character thinks and feels without stating it. Subtext is the unspoken that occurs when a person has something at stake. It is a delicate art, since it is what characters are saying between the lines. Between lovers, it can be amazingly sexy; during an argument it can bring in an extra layer of tension.

Dialogue that is directly about the issue at hand is called "on the nose" dialogue. If your story is made up of only on the nose dialogue it will lack subtlety. Characters speak directly and honestly when they feel safe as when they're talking to a best friend or therapist. Often other exchanges are more slippery.

To use subtext in your dialogue, insert exchanges that have double meanings. You can also use action, such as when a character turns away and starts fiddling with an object, indicating discomfort. Or a character might change the subject and evade questions. A character can blush, stammer, choke on a response, or become rigid. Silence can also be a means of using subtext, as is answering a question with another question.

Hollywood script doctor and author of *Creating Unforgettable Characters*, Linda Seger explains subtext:

> Often characters don't understand themselves. They're often not direct and don't say what they mean. We might say that the subtext is all the underlying drives and meanings that are not apparent to the character, but that are apparent to the audience or reader.

Nonfiction Question:

Every word you write delivers a message and casts a spell on your reader. But in crafting nonfiction, the writer walks a tightrope, writing in a voice and style that is accessible, but not intrusive. Subtlety often means to imply rather than announce, to reveal rather than instruct. It's a technique that falls under the "show, don't tell" dictum. When you write with subtlety and restraint, you are including the reader as your collaborator.

In *Make Your Words Work*, Gary Provost writes:

> Being subtle in your stories and articles means much more than just avoiding overstatement. And showing often means letting the reader look into his own life experience. Subtlety is at the heart of the relationship between the writer and the reader. The extent to which you are subtle is the extent to which you allow the reader to collaborate on your story, to fill in the blanks.

A woman with blazing red nails and lips, wearing a gold lamé dress that looks like it's painted on, spells siren. You don't need to tell the reader that she's trying to appear seductive; her appearance says it all. Don't tell the reader that someone is sad when you depict tears rolling down her cheeks. Tears paint the picture. Many techniques can create subtlety. For instance, don't shout at the reader with exclamation points; avoid using all-capital words, excess parenthesis, boldface, or italics. Readers can infer the meaning in important words.

The Writer's Path:

All writers entertain doubts. But what is doubt all about? In *It's Easier Than You Think*, Sylvia Boorstein describes doubt from a Buddhist perspective, calling it "slippery" among destructive thinking patterns because it's not connected to a strong body sensation like lust or anger.

She writes:

> Doubt ... slips into the mind disguised as demoralizing thoughts. Once past the security gate of mindfulness, doubt acts like an undercover agent, sabotaging faith and trust. It can blithely undermine confidence on all levels, because it does it entirely as an inside job.

She closes the chapter by describing a morning when she was demoralized, sad, and wracked with doubts. And then she describes how a few hours later her pain simply disappeared. "Doubt had rolled in and rolled out, like a thunderstorm."

So give your doubt an audience, listen to the thunder. But remember, it is only thunder. Comfort yourself as you'd comfort a child in the midst of a crashing storm. Then let the storm pass, and write again.

———

58. Joy: Lake/Lake

You must stay drunk on writing so reality cannot destroy you.

—Ray Bradbury

The waters in the lake are a place of quiet, abundance, and nurturance. Translated, this means that your goals have a great chance for success, especially when you receive encouragement from others and encourage them. Optimism, inspiration, and ease in communicating are the essence of Hexagram 58.

If you are a public speaker, this is a terrific time for speaking engagements, meetings, and general communications about your work. Share your ideas and allow others to offer opinions and suggestions. Use your leadership skills to encourage others. This is not a time for self-sufficiency, but neither should you be dependent on other people's opinions. Trust in yourself and spread goodwill.

In all your relationships, strive for deeper communication and generosity. In fact, compassion, gentleness, and diplomacy are required in all your interactions. If you have criticisms or harsh opinions, this is not the time to air them.

Fiction Question:

What is genuinely odd about reading fiction is that we are essentially following an account of a character's misfortune. While in real life we strive for happiness and peace, fiction is the opposite of real life. Fictional characters are depicted struggling toward a goal in scenes that are embroidered with tension and strife, as they barely survive failures, setbacks, and heartbreaks.

Most commercial novels describe a happy ending, but the story events that lead you to that moment portray misery piled on top of misery. Characters suffer because readers empathize when they suffer, and stayed glued to the scene. Author Jack Bickham recommends:

> Let your character relax, feel happy and content, and be worried about nothing, and your story dies. Pour on all sorts of woes so your poor character is thoroughly miserable and in the deepest kind of trouble, and your story perks right up— along with your reader's interest.

Thus, when you write about happy times in fiction, you must do so with great care. Happy moments or periods of normalcy are most often used as a means of pacing. Often, these moments are fleeting, foreshadow the ending, or disclose what the protagonist is fighting for.

An example of writing about happiness is found in Peter Robinson's series featuring police detectives Alan Banks and Annie Cabbot. In *Playing with Fire*, the story begins with two barges ablaze on an empty canal. On board are the blackened remains of the two inhabitants. As the investigation gets underway, there is an evening when the detectives take a breather. Cabbot is out on a date at a posh restaurant and Banks is home enjoying a relaxing evening with Scotch and a video. But the reprieve doesn't last, because another fire is set and they are called to a muddy field and the smoldering wreckage of a mobile home. In the midst of calm, the cell phone jangles and sends them back into the labyrinth of the murder investigation. However, Banks' quiet evening at home and Cabbot's dinner date serve as a potent contrast to the horrors of a murder case and give the reader the sort of roller coaster ride that is so delicious in fiction. Likewise, create quiet times in your stories, but also find ways to disrupt lighter moments and create a world of disquiet and movement.

Nonfiction Question:

Nonfiction writers often write about pain, struggles, and secrets, but joy is another rich landscape, ripe for exploration. And the simpler the joys, the more they mean to us.

In an early scene in the movie *The Sound of Music,* Maria, the new governess, is calming the von Trapp children during a thunderstorm by trilling "My Favorite Things." The song is a charming recitation of the nun's means to distract herself from her troubles—raindrops on roses, whiskers on kittens.

Most adults require soothing from time to time, and we need to be reminded of what lifts our hearts. This practice can be as simple as keeping a list of the large and small things that make you happy. Every list will be different. Perhaps yours will include bathing by candlelight, the sound of soft rain on the roof, receiving a letter from an old friend, working in your flower garden amid the morning dew, or dancing to Motown. Perhaps it includes pizza, chocolate mousse, bread pudding, or the memory of your Aunt Ellen's kitchen during the holidays. Perhaps you love horseback riding, bicycle riding, or your vintage Harley. Small joys, so individual and instructive, are a terrific source for writing and a balm when your writing routine feels flat.

Take a few minutes and make the joy list. It will calm, reveal, and revive.

The Writer's Path:

Many qualities are necessary for the writing path, but one trait that is seldom discussed is generosity. Nothing can help a beginning writer more than encouragement from a fellow writer, especially one who has achieved some success.

Writing is often a lonely occupation. As if isolated on the raft of creativity amid a turbulent ocean, you struggle with words and ideas, plots and themes. Alone. At times this isolation makes you feel apart from the world, even abandoned. To break through this isolation, you need fellow writers who understand the process and the sacrifices made. And then you need to return the favor. Writers are required to have a generosity of spirit, a willingness to lend an ear, perhaps to help out when a friend is struggling with a sagging plot. It all boils down to this simple fact: generosity given is generosity returned.

Author Elizabeth Berg weighs in on the subject:

> People who support you in the right way make you feel really good about writing. They give you encouragement without sounding false. They try hard not to be resentful of the time

you need to take away from them to write. Also—and this is critical—they make you feel that you will do even better. That's not because they like what they're seeing now; rather, it's because they like what they're seeing enough to believe that you're in this for the long haul, and that you will continue to grow and improve as a writer.

59. Easing: Wind/Water

Find out the reason that commands you to write;
see whether it has spread its roots into the very depth of your heart;
confess to yourself whether you would have to die
if you were forbidden to write.

—Rainer Maria Rilke

The wind is blowing over the soft waters, creating turbulence and shaking things up for the good of all. In long-ago China this hexagram was illustrated by the emperor entering the ancestral hall to offer respect and prayers, asking for protection for his people. This gesture brought luck and good omens.

Under the auspices of Hexagram 59, it's a powerful time to start new projects and overcome writer's block. Jump in with a strong sense of purpose and focus on the big picture. Pay homage to ancient wisdom, myths, and symbols, and notice how they inspire you and others. Remember your responsibility to society at large.

Resolve disagreements and clarify matters now. Approach problems, and especially problem people, with a gentle heart and compassion. If you har-

bor grudges or resentments, let them go. If you are involved in power struggles, solve them tactfully and move on. It is a time for harmony, not
struggles. Look inward and renew your spirituality. This is a profound time
for knowing and trusting yourself and your instincts.

Fiction Question:

People evolved stories over time as a way to explore what it means to be
human. These stories, first told around a fire, explained the origin of the
earth, spoke of the beasts roaming the forests, and described how the gods
shaped the affairs of humankind. But mostly stories told throughout time
were attempts to explain the human family and were rich explorations that
stimulate the imagination.

In order to enrapture your audience and bring to life these timeless themes,
learn basic storytelling techniques. Study the three-act structure of fiction that
has been around since Aristotle wrote *The Poetics*. The three acts, also called
the beginning, middle, and ending, are the set up, complication, and resolution. Once you understand this basic structure, examine the broader strokes of
your story. Make sure that you've written for all the senses and that the details, descriptions, and scenes contribute to the overall story line and the
fictional world. Details are included to stir the reader's emotions, shape a believable fictional world, create people whom we come to know intimately, and
push the story forward. Don't insert details merely because you can.

Do not write plots that contain coincidences, contrivances, or the cavalry
saving the day. Protagonists solve problems with some help from other characters, but mostly through self-reliance and personal growth.

Beware of needless flashbacks. Flashbacks must always be vital to the overall plot, and as vivid and brief as possible. Because they stop the forward
momentum of the plot, you need a good reason to abandon the straight-ahead

chronology.

Never include characters without names or include characters simply for the sake of populating your story world. All characters have a purpose in the story and scene.

Don't create a plot in which the antagonist falters in order for the protagonist to win. In the best stories, the protagonist outwits the antagonist, prodded by desperation, desire, and will.

Unless it is the only logical way to end a story, such as when writing a thriller, avoid writing a climax with a car chase, earthquake or other violent act of nature, bombs, or other incendiary devices. Instead, write an ending that the reader cannot see coming, but at the same time is the perfect wrap-up for the story.

Nonfiction Question:

Symbols and patterns have always inspired writers. One source for nonfiction writers is to read the journals that you've kept over the years. In these pages, you'll find your attempts to understand your world, but you'll also discover themes, patterns, and seismic shifts of thinking.

As you read through your journals, search for recurring words, images, events, issues, and problems. Although you'll also find complaints and venting, the pages contain key moments and awarenesses that expose your inner life.

Because a journal is an unfolding story with the ending yet to be written, the underlying themes are often apparent only after you write them. Also, when in the midst of struggling through a trying situation, you often cannot see it clearly because you're too busy trying to survive. Understanding only arrives later when matters are resolved and your emotions have cooled. Your job is to discover these insights along with what has mattered in your life, especially noticing your connections, including frayed ones.

Look for omens or symbols that moved you. Notice how you handled difficult transitions and reached important decisions. Examine the topics that you kept returning to. Notice your mistakes and regrets, but try to join them to larger themes and patterns in your life.

If you have not kept journals, another method is to spend time creating a list of key events in your life. As when examining your journals, try to understand the larger meanings and ramifications behind these important incidents.

The Writer's Path:

It is time to address the tyranny of perfectionism. Perfectionism is the bane of many writers and is often the culprit in writer's block. You know you suffer from perfectionism if you fret endlessly while writing, can never stop editing, and are never satisfied with anything you write.

In *Bird by Bird* Anne Lamott considers it such an important topic that she devotes an entire chapter to it. She writes:

> Perfectionism is the voice of the oppressor, the enemy of the people… Perfectionism will ruin your writing, blocking inventiveness and playfulness and life force…. Perfectionism means that you try desperately not to leave so much mess to clean up. But clutter and mess show us that life is being lived. Clutter is wonderfully fertile ground—you can still discover new treasures under all those piles, clean things up, edit things out, fix things, get a grip. Tidiness suggests that something is as good as it's going to get. Tidiness makes me think of held breath, of suspended animation, while writing needs to breathe and move.

It's essential to determine if you are a perfectionist or if you are merely striving to write better. A perfectionist sets impossible standards; a healthy person sets high ones. A perfectionist is never satisfied with his work; a healthy person enjoys the process and the outcome. A perfectionist sees his mistakes as personal failures; a healthy person sees mistakes as opportunities to improve. A perfectionist has problems receiving criticism; a healthy person welcomes criticism.

Perfectionism leads to depression, anxiety, and obsessive thoughts. Find a way out of this trap through compassion toward yourself and all your efforts. Learn how to be realistic about what you can accomplish at this stage in your writing career, and give yourself permission to experiment.

---

60. Self-Control: Water/Lake

When there are no words, a glance is enough.

—Gustave Flaubert

Hexagram 60 has a number of meanings and was originally depicted by a section of a bamboo stalk. Its meaning—restriction—is the opposite of the previous hexagram that talks about dispersing. Limits exist in nature, as when summer gives way to autumn, then winter. And laws, a form of limitations, were created by all societies to preserve order.

It is also necessary to apply limits to the self. Create realistic limits and systems to stay focused. The artist who remains balanced and disciplined amid hard work is the artist who accomplishes his goals. If you overreach now or indulge in emotional extremes, you'll pay the price. Avoid both extravagance and miserliness. It all comes down to balance in actions, thoughts, and emotions.

Goals become reality when sensible plans are put in place. If you have grandiose dreams for your career, now is the time to make careful choices. If the length or scope of your project seems overwhelming, focus on it one paragraph at a time. Accept the reality that you might not finish every project that visits your imagination. Instead, commit to the ones that hold the most promise and are within your capabilities. Within this focus, adhere to your values and principles.

Don't expect too much from other people; accept people for who they are instead of who you wish they were. If a relationship is floundering, create ground rules that you can both agree on. Don't lock yourself away in isolation. Socialize to recharge your batteries, but don't spend time with people to avoid writing.

Fiction Question:

Writing about emotions takes finesse and restraint, but it also requires that you spark your reader's imagination, not do the work for him. While most fiction is designed to stir the emotions, deliver emotions without being shrill or overstated.

There is a way to write about jealousy, betrayal, grief, misery, greed—the whole gamut of strong emotions—without shrieking at the reader. One guideline: in the most emotionally charged situations, use the subtlest approach. Search for a single, poignant image as a stand-in for a whole gamut of feelings. Be guided by the old line, "Don't tell me about the tragedy of war; instead show me the child's shoe discarded by the side of the road." There is huge power in understatement, in the bedroom door that remains closed for hours in the middle of the day.

Examine how the masters handle strong sentiments. In the epilogue of *Peace Like a River,* Leif Enger cryptically describes his brother's forced, lifetime exile from the family. "Exile has its hollow hours. Some years I've noticed odd tilts in his speech. No doubt he has lived among accents, I hope in pleasant places, but he tells me painfully little. He asks and asks." These brief sentences are wrung from grief and longing, but the reader feels them without being clobbered by them.

Nonfiction Question:

Wordiness is a turn-off. The more verbose the writing, the less likely it is that someone will read it. Wordiness bores, confuses, and tires the reader. A wordy draft reveals not only a lack of editing but also a lack of consideration for the reader. It is often mired in jargon, purple prose, clichés, and modifiers, written with the false belief that the subject demands many words.

Any word that doesn't add to the meaning of your sentence actually detracts from it. So as you edit, don't be afraid to strip your sentences down to their cleanest components. If this process is painful, remember that you can always garnish sentences with modifiers and metaphors in your final draft when you strive to enhance the themes.

One helpful tip for trimming excess is to rid your sentences of "little word pile up" that clutters them. For example, instead of "The scout troop planned to go to the performance that would be held on Friday a little before 6:00," write "The troop planned to attend Friday's performance just before 6:00."

The Writer's Path:

There will never be enough minutes, hours, or days to accomplish all your writing dreams. While this might sound harsh, the truth is that setting limits allows you to tap your creative potential. This doesn't mean that you can only work on one project at a time; many writers work best when more than one pot is boiling. But choose wisely when you select the project that demands most of your energy, and reserve your peak hours for working on this main project.

However, also keep a "tomorrow" file for sudden ideas and inspirations that sometimes sweep into your thoughts. If you note these ideas briefly and stow them in a safe place, they won't drown out your current progress.

—

61. Inner Truth: Wind/Lake

So this is always the key: you have to write
the book you love, the book that's alive in your heart.
That's the one you have to write.

—Lurleen McDaniel

Inner Truth implies a good omen and traditional images for this hexagram represent fishes swimming. Some *I Ching* texts describe the water as the Great River or the stream of life, while others point out that the fish are swimming in shallows and ponds. These fish, believed to be lucky, suggest that the time is ripe to move into new territory. Before venturing out, examine the path (or stream) ahead, gather information, and believe in yourself.

Explore the deeper meaning in this hexagram, which is how truth works in your life. On one hand, Hexagram 61 asserts that the truth will set you free. On the other hand, it reminds you to understand other people's truths. Listen carefully now with an open mind and speak directly from your heart. True and lasting relationships are based on honesty.

This hexagram also reminds you to remain true to your self and your dreams. Stand up for the truth in all your dealings, no matter the price. However, don't invite conflict. Apply the wisdom you've earned with skill and care. Genuine insight will penetrate any difficulties.

Fiction Question:

Readers read novels for the pleasures of living among the characters' lives, for becoming intimately acquainted with people they could not meet in ordinary life. This sort of intimacy is deliciously involving, and often requires that the reader understands how the character thinks. Introspection, and a character's thoughts in general, can offer powerful insights into that person. But when using these thoughts, small flashes go a long way to reveal him.

Characters are defined when they're struggling with difficult decisions and choices. In fact, many stories are about a character impaled on the horns of a dilemma, particularly a moral dilemma. The reader watches him weigh the sides, often trying to avoid the consequences. But this weighing and worrying must not be spelled out as plainly as a teacher writing on a blackboard.

A character's thoughts cannot serve as a shortcut to characterization or take the place of drama. We know characters best when they act, when they talk, when they plunge in. Be especially careful of weaving thoughts into action. In general, stick with the action and save thoughts and introspection for the sequel moments—the quieter times when the action has subsided and emotional reactions are called for.

Nonfiction Question:

Tim O'Brien, the author of a memoir and novels, including *The Things They Carried* based on his tour of duty in Vietnam, wrote:

> Stories are for joining the past to the future. Stories are for those late hours in the night when you can't remember how you got from where you were to where you are. Stories are for eternity, when memory is erased, when there is nothing to remember except the story.

In your search to tell the truth of your life, remember that there is nothing to remember except the truth. The best literary nonfiction doesn't *add* to life; it conveys a life that was already there. You are adding artful touches, not wholesale events. Fiction is about fabricated events; nonfiction finds the meaning in real life events. Your story is a place where human drama, truth, and imagination intersect, brought to life using creativity and writing skills. As O'Brien says, it "comes down to gut instinct. A true war story, if truly told, makes the stomach believe." Truth always makes the stomach believe.

The Writer's Path:

Contemplate what it means to be true to yourself and your dreams. In this contemplation, think about the things, people, and places that you love. If you write about what you love, your writing will have profound implications and will reveal the truth of who you are.

Find what you love: baseball, opera, sunsets at the shore, rain forests, Volkswagen vans, or noir detective films. Follow what you love to a lakeside dock and a Douglas fir forest shimmering in the afternoon sunlight. Notice your grandfather's scarred farmer's hands, and note what he taught you about soil and hard work and paying attention to weather. Recall how your grandmother taught you how to cream sugar and butter together to concoct fairy-light pastries. Notice what you collect: crystals, baseball cards, jokes, antique plates, old cars, or vintage tools.

What we love defines us, paints our soul for the world to see.

Yes, there are shattering truths and harsh realities that deserve writing about. But what you love is the larger truth of your life.

62. Attention to Detail: Thunder/Mountain

Six: The 64 Hexagrams

No ideas but in things.

—William Carlos Williams

With thunder over the mountain, the mountain blocks the sound of thunder crashing. A symbol connected to this hexagram is of a bird carrying a message. This generally portrays a good omen for your affairs, along with a reminder that attending to details creates success. It is vital to be conscientious in all your dealings now. Do not leap, hurry, or take shortcuts; instead, proceed one small step after another. In this careful manner, if a change is called for, it will be easy to make adjustments. It's also a good time to keep a low profile and not force your will on another person.

A transition is underway, so remain dignified and rein in your emotions. However, this transition does not involve a dramatic change, basking in the limelight, taking risks, or new beginnings. Understand that sometimes things are at a low ebb. Adjust to these factors with grace and patience, and pay attention to everyday affairs so that your life hums along.

Be frugal and pay attention to money matters when you choose this hexagram. Adjust your daily habits and routines so that you get the writing done. Avoid gambles and grandiose fantasies. Modest gains are still gains, and you can write a book one word, one page at a time.

Fiction Question:

Descriptive details trigger the reader's imagination and paint places, people, events, and wonders onto the page. Events, action, or dialogue push a story forward, but descriptive details assure the reader of their reality.

Yet choosing just the right details is no easy matter. Since description is static, it must be inserted sparingly and if possible, create a mood in the scene. If you constantly stop your story to describe sunsets, seashores, interiors, hairstyles, or heartbeats, it will lose its momentum. If possible, put description in motion through a character's viewpoint, amid action scenes, in the middle of dialogue, or while characters are in motion.

Description should appear natural, never a list or inventory, never an afterthought. Deliver details to the reader through all the senses, like ice in a glass or the sweat on a character's upper lip. A detail can be the color of the institutional beige walls, a cornflower blue sky, or a gaudy bouquet. It can be the musky smells that linger on the sheets after lovemaking, or a baby's skin compared to the "feel of white tea roses, the rising scent of warm cornbread," in "Stars at Elbow and Foot" by Amy Bloom.

Description can be daring, such as a protagonist who wears a black rubber dress; it can dazzle the reader, as in the horrific details of a murder scene or the opulence of a grand ball; or it can be magical, like the quidditch matches in J.K. Rowling's Harry Potter series.

But mostly descriptive details should be crucial to the overall story. Description illuminates themes and key moments, is always necessary and revealing, and is never extraneous.

Nonfiction Question:

Writing is in the details. In nonfiction, descriptive details grant the piece authority, and also make the experiences poignant, sensory, and alive. Choose details that are so vital that the piece would suffer without them. Details should affect the outcome and make readers understand theme and meaning.

The issue of when to include or leave out details is something that every writer wrestles with. Start with the obvious: when the essay, article, or story first forms in your imagination, pay attention to the first images that come to you. Next, notice the images that evoke emotions, the ones that make you angry, sad, or confused.

Description is accurate and precise, used by a writer the way a surgeon wields a scalpel. When you edit and rewrite, separate the necessary details from the purple prose. In general, use restraint with descriptive details, inserting only small bits at a time, not long paragraphs or pages, because description is static and stops the action and forward movement.

Professor Lauren Kessler, author of ten books, explains:

> As readers, we understand the tremendous importance of the keenly observed, well-presented detail. Writing succeeds when it puts pictures inside our head, when it makes it possible for us to visualize people and landscapes, actions and scenes. We remember what we can visualize. We think about what we can remember...
>
> Details are the small particulars that make up the whole, the discrete components that define, describe and individualize. In nonfiction, detail is neither invented nor imagined. It is observed directly from real life, the product of attentive and extensive research. The precise and intelligent choice detail creates and sharpens images in the reader's mind.

The Writer's Path:

Description begins with the writer. You cannot insert compelling details into your prose unless you have noticed these details in your own life. Collect, gather, cultivate, and observe all the nuance of life, including nature, weather, and lighting. Ask yourself about the people you know and meet and see on the street. Notice personality traits, quirky behaviors, gestures, posture, and body movements. Remember or record conversations, jokes, and quips. Jot notes on what you read, what plays you attend, and what films you watch.

In *Page After Page*, Heather Sellers says that the tools that a writer really needs are free and one of these tools is an observant heart. So notice your world, and use your heart in this noticing.

—

63. The Finish Line: Water/Fire

Your past is not your potential.
In any hour you can choose to liberate the future.

— Marilyn Ferguson

The early Chinese symbols for this hexagram portrayed a person who had just finished eating a meal. Images from later centuries were of three people pulling together to steer a boat past an obstacle. The structure of The Finish Line—water flowing downward and fire licking upward—combine for a positive outcome, as when fire heats water to a boil. This image means that the situation is favorable, and possibly perfect.

Sometimes a race is lost in the final seconds because the front-runner grows complacent or has not noticed a rival gaining on him. You're close to the end here, and only need to fine-tune and fill in with finishing flourishes. But as you near the end, stay focused, alert, and attentive to details. If your current situation brings a surprise or an unanticipated change, adapt quickly.

Because this final stage must be completed for you to move on to a new phase, don't rush or become slipshod. Hexagram 63 suggests that you prepare yourself for this ending long before it arrives. It also advises that you remain balanced through every phase of life, but especially when you're near the finish line. Problems might still crop up, so anticipate them and your prudent reactions.

If you can remain calm and thoughtful now, success is certain. Profitable outcomes and true insights are possible. You are in the right place at the right time—keep moving.

Fiction Question:

A true epilogue is set off from the plot in time and place, and is created for a specific purpose. An example is found in Michael Crichton's *Jurassic Park*, where the epilogue comes after the survivors have left the island and the dinosaur theme park is destroyed.

The epilogue is part of the denouement, a term that means the untying or unraveling of the plot. In the epilogue the reader learns the consequences of the plot and necessary information such as the fate of the characters. This information was not revealed in the climax, so it provides a final wrap-up and looks back on the story events. An effectively constructed epilogue does not carry on too long or it will seem anticlimactic.

An epilogue can be written in a significantly different style, such as a letter or journal entry, or come from another character's point of view. When crafting an epilogue, keep in mind that you're relating the consequences or results of the story, but at the same time, you're not revealing so much that the reader cannot surmise what has happened. John Irving writes: "An epilogue is more than a body count. An epilogue, in the disguise of wrapping up the past, is really a way of warning us about the future."

Nonfiction Question:

The best essay endings linger in the reader's imagination. The lead of your essay has made a promise to the reader; your ending proves that you have kept this promise. Because readers tend to remember endings, it's important to carefully choose among the techniques in your writing toolbox. Work at creating an ending that unifies the whole. It cannot veer wildly from the tone and style that went before.

No matter the subject, resist the urge to preach or climb onto a soapbox. Instead, consider circling back to your theme or the opening to emphasize important points or images.

Use an anecdote, a small scene, a dramatic moment, or a dialogue exchange to create significance. Or find a single poignant detail similar to a snapshot that serves as shorthand for larger issues. You might try writing a surprise ending, as long as the surprise is not a bombshell and foreshadowing prepares the reader for it. Endings often work best when the writer discloses an emotion that supports the theme of the piece. Depending on the tone and purpose of the essay or memoir, the best endings leave the reader musing and thoughtfully evaluating the whole.

The Writer's Path:

Here is the bottom line: most writers will write their first book while working full time, juggling family obligations, and attending to the details of life. Your car requires gas and oil, the refrigerator must be stocked, the laundry attended to. Throw in exercise, reading, volunteering, a spiritual practice, and friendships. With so many obligations, and the undeniable fact that writing requires a large commitment of time, balance is called for.

But how do you achieve balance? By keeping the writing a priority and not taking on too much outside of your writing routine. If you're in the midst of writing a novel, it is not the best time to remodel the kitchen, run a marathon, or landscape the yard. Instead, work on small beautifying projects or improvements and conserve your energy for writing. You want to lose fifty pounds? It's a terrific goal, but one that must be incorporated within the writing life. For example, for every hour that you're sitting at your desk, plan to counteract this sedentary routine with five to fifteen minutes spent exercising. It's not the right time to rise at dawn and work out for two hours, then settle in to write. It's a time to make tough choices and put writing first while slipping in small improvements.

---

64. Near the End: Fire / Water

Books aren't written—they're rewritten. Including your own.
It is one of the hardest things to accept,
especially after the seventh rewrite hasn't quite done it.

—Michael Crichton

Imagine a rushing stream that contains a shallow spot where you can ford with safety. This is that place. But it is crucial that you cross only at this specific location, and that you don't misstep. Applying this to your life, no matter what is going on now, don't let down your guard or employ half-hearted efforts. Take your time and don't take anything or anyone for granted.

Hexagram 64 indicates that you're near the end of a project or goal. With the end in sight, don't celebrate too soon or become sloppy. Even if you're running out of steam, this phase calls for street smarts. You will likely be tested just when you're certain that you're out of the woods. Centered and wary will get you through this period.

Clarity, determination, and honesty will also see you through and bring success. If you are involved in a get-rich-quick scheme or shady deal, bail out before it's too late.

Another powerful aspect of a dwindling cycle is that while it winds down, a rebirth is taking place. In every ending lies a beginning, and the sweet seeds of newness are already planted. This is the Tao manifest in all things.

Fiction Question:

At last you're ready for the final edit of your manuscript. It's possible that the scrutinizing and fine-tuning called for now are the most difficult parts of the process. It's also likely that you're weary of your words, characters, and writing in general. Take heart and find a way to accomplish this most necessary task.

First, create conditions for success. Print it out and read it in a place other than your normal workplace. Read it when you feel fresh and optimistic, not when you're tired or cranky. With a red pen in hand, notice typos, misplaced words, and awkward phrasing.

Attempt to see the big picture now. Does each scene contain a goal? Are the subplots tied up? Have your characters' core traits been revealed? Is there a forward momentum throughout? Is there a cohesive voice and tone throughout? Is the dialogue tight and underlined with tension? Does it sound natural, or are characters giving speeches? Is the point of view consistent and does each scene contain visual details so that the reader can envision the time and place?

Don't hurry the final edit. Be prepared for the rush of emotions that you'll feel during this stage. If you despair, find ways to cope. If you're still confused, seek help.

Nonfiction Question:

Annie Dillard warns writers not to fall in love with their own words because they take on " a necessary quality, the ring of the inevitable." The purpose of the first draft is to provide a canvas for the second draft, which then provides material for later drafts.

But as you work on your final draft, you also confront the hardest decisions and choices. You're faced with this hard reality: often, your first ideas are not your best ones. While working on this draft, ask yourself if this is truly the best course, and be prepared to sometimes reject your earliest approach. In the final draft you're attempting to see the work from an emotional distance so that, when viewed with dispassion, it creates a richer, more meaningful approach.

The Writer's Path:

Hexagram 64 reminds the questioner that the work is not yet done. The symbol for Near the End is a tree with branches that have not yet extended to their full growth. You are midway or nearing the end, with more to learn and attain. Instead of surrendering, look behind you and congratulate yourself on how far you've come. Reflect on the past in light of the present. Take stock of your successes and realize that they are the seeds for your next steps and accomplishments. Notice how when you buckled down and stuck to your writing routine, the word count grew and your ideas flowed better.

Crossing the Bridge

So here you have it. The ancient symbols and archetypes created thousands of years ago by sages who wished to help others travel life's highway and the bridge that connects this wisdom to your writing practice and quandaries. Sometimes when writers start out to write a novel or any daunting project, it seems that the gap between their beginning efforts and the ending of their story or getting published is as vast as the Grand Canyon. Beginners especially worry that the obstacles to writing are too many, the techniques needed to write too complicated, and the discipline required too difficult to harness. But writing is a skill; that like carpentry or cooking can be learned and improved on with practice. When you write, you are joining legions of people throughout time who needed to comment and bear witness and tell stories.

If you are person who was attracted to this book because it represents another way of knowing the self and working with energy, it's likely that you're open to many ways of seeing the world and its possibilities and miracles. Keep your mind open when you write and stay calm in the midst of all aspects of the process. It is possible to take your place among the writers from the past and the writers who are now infusing their magic onto the page. It's a grand way to spend a life, or to perhaps occupy only a part of your weeks and months and years. When you choose writing, so much is possible, so many techniques can be mastered with diligence and attention. If you have never started writing, or have given up along the way and have been gazing with longing or confusion across the canyon, simply begin and have faith. And use *The Writers I Ching* to provide a bridge across that massive canyon, to find along the way a mentor, a helper, a soothing voice.